FIRST DAYS OF PARENTING

FIRST DAYS OF PARENTING

DEVOTIONS TO CELEBRATE YOUR NEW ARRIVAL

Mary Harwell Sayler

BROADMAN & HOLMAN PUBLISHERS

Nashville, Tennessee

© 1995
by MARY HARWELL SAYLER
All rights reserved
Printed in the United States of America

4253-83
0-8054-5383-0

Dewey Decimal Classification: 242.645
Subject Heading: Devotional Literature \ Parenting
Library of Congress Card Catalog Number: 94-42412

Library of Congress Cataloging-in-Publication Data

Sayler, Mary Harwell
    First days of parenting : devotions to celebrate your new arrival / by Mary Harwell Sayler.
       p. cm.
    ISBN 0-8054-5383-0
    1. Parents—Prayer-books and devotions—English. 2. Devotional calendars. 3. Spiritual life—Christianity. I. Title.
  BV4845.S28   1995
  242'.645—dc20   94-42412
                                                                  CIP

*In loving memory of my father,
Horace Ewing Harwell,
whose empathy, good humor,
and faith in God and people
prepared the way
for me to know and love
my Heavenly Father,
I give thanks.*

*I'm especially grateful
for my dad's uncommonly
good sense in committing
his life to Christ,
his church and family,
and the "angel" he always loved,
my mother, Mildred Angel Harwell.*

*May their descendants
—and yours—
live in love
throughout eternity.*

Introduction

When you first learned you were expecting a baby—or first received approval to adopt—did you ever imagine that *you* would be the one being born? Well, congratulations! You have just given birth to parenthood!

With the birth of a first child, at least one new parent comes into the world. Even if pregnancy or adoption was especially difficult, the *hard* part begins as new mothers or fathers ask, "What do I do now?"

Fortunately, God has not left you orphaned in this task. He has given you guidance through His Word and through the wisdom of those who've gone before. Nonetheless, you will be faced with numerous questions and challenges in this new phase of your lives. The devotions here will offer practical as well as spiritual advice to help you learn and grow in your new roles.

Some devotions will relate more to mothers and some to fathers, but all will help you through these first days. You may choose to read them separately or together. And they will begin with the days just before the birth of your new child or the time just before an adopted child comes to live with and be part of your family. Each devotion contains a Scripture passage, prayer, and devotional comments. You'll also find space to journal as you begin this new phase of your journey with God.

His Word will guide your first days of parenting and continue on, long after this book ends. So, from the start, become a child yourself in His Spirit as you seek godly

First Days of Parenting

truths in the translation of the Bible which most reveals itself to you.

In this book, Scriptures come to you from the versions often used in church services or Bible study groups. They're shown as follows:

KJV = *King James Version*—English translation authorized by King James of England.

NCV = Scriptures quoted from *New Century Version*, copyright © 1991 by Word Publishing, Dallas, Texas 75039. Used by permission.

NIV = Scripture taken from the *Holy Bible, New International Version*, copyright © 1973, 1978, 1984, International Bible Society. Used by permission of Zondervan Bible Publishers.

NRSV = *New Revised Standard Version Bible*, copyright © 1989, Division of Christian Education of the National Council of the Churches of Christ in the United States of America.

*For you created my inmost being;
you knit me together
in my mother's womb.*

Psalm 139:13, NIV

Congratulations! You're becoming part of a new life—your baby's, of course, but also your own life as a brand new parent! So, are you ready to become a real-live person's newly born mom or dad? Probably not. No one really is! But, hopefully, you've planned for this special moment, feel happy about its timing, and have enjoyed the attention that a first pregnancy or adoption often brings.

Once morning sickness has subsided to a mere memory, many expectant parents find they're closer to each other, despite the extra padding in between! However, if you're alone or had not yet expected to be expecting, just expect some unsettling emotions now!

Under the most ideal conditions, changes do occur. Moods swing. Tummies curve into lap trays. Fears balloon out of proportion; and worries about your ability, background, and budget begin to bulge. Even if you eagerly await your baby's arrival, your whole world has suddenly turned upside down!

Isn't it terrific? The very position that prepares your child's natural entrance into the birth canal also prepares you for a debut as a parent! Remember how the doctor said the preferable way for babies to be born is head first? Well,

First Days of Parenting

as you prep for this wondrously blessed event, having your life turned upside down helps you to come *head first* into the world of parenthood with Jesus Christ as the Head.

Prayer: Dear Heavenly Father, I'm excited about the baby, but I'm scared too. Everything I've known and worked for suddenly seems reversed, and I'm not at all sure I'm ready! But You're the Creator of love and life, not I! Help me to draw closer to You, Lord. Help me to trust You to bring into being all that You've begun in Jesus' name.

Journey with God: In the space below, talk with God about your fears, faith, and feelings. Ask Him to prepare your body, mind, and spirit for a joyful entry into parenthood.

_____

_____

_____

_____

_____

_____

_____

_____

_____

First Days of Parenting

Day 2

They said to her, "None of your relatives has this name." Then they began motioning to his father to find out what name he wanted to give him.

Luke 1:61–62, NRSV

Have you picked out a name yet? Most parents begin to discuss the topic at least nine months before they fill out a birth certificate! Some wait to see signs of their baby's personality before they decide what to call their child. Some even pray about each name that comes to mind. Unless God has a specific reason, such as fulfilling a prophetic word, He probably won't insist on a certain name, but family members might! They may say something like, "I was hoping you'd name the baby after me." Or, "Are you nuts? Why would anybody want to call a kid by *that* name?"

The naming of names is a personal matter. Some names make you think of people you don't like too much while others help you recall favorite family members or friends. Some names seem pleasant but could eventually become tiresome. Others sound cute for a baby but infantile for an adult!

If you haven't yet decided, say aloud the names you've liked for a while and listen to their sounds. Pretend to call a child and an adult by that name. Also, look up the meaning or origin to see if this has any significance for you. For instance, Alice means "truth." Kirk means "of the church."

Think about biblical names too. If you enjoyed hearing about a Bible character, such as Caleb, Joshua, Miriam, or Ruth, consider naming your baby after such a person. In God's Word, you'll find lots of interesting choices—from Adam to Zechariah or Abigail to Zipporah! Yet God leaves this last word on the naming of names up to you!

Prayer: Thank You, Lord, for letting us choose our baby's name. Each has connotations or a story behind it that we might not know, but You do! Help us to pick a name that's pleasing to You and appropriate for our child in the name of Your Chosen One, Jesus Christ.

Journey with God: Discuss your baby's and your own names with God. Ask Him to help you hear Him, calling you.

> *Jesus said,*
> *"Let the little children come to me,*
> *and do not hinder them,*
> *for the kingdom of heaven belongs*
> *to such as these."*
>
> Matthew 19:14, NIV

As your baby's birth draws near, you might be deluged with gifts! Your coworkers, friends, family, or spouse might shower you with so much attention, you don't want it to end. If so, praise God for your condition! A loving, supportive environment helps to nurture your baby's health and also your development as a parent.

But maybe you're all alone. Maybe your "significant other" helped to produce this significant change in your life and hasn't been heard from since! Maybe you're a single parent, ready to adopt, or an unwed father with a newborn on your hands—hands that suddenly seem to have five sets of thumbs!

Prenatal conditions vary from person to person, but God and His Word do not. No matter what circumstances you're in, He's faithful in showering His love. He surrounds you with His presence in the nurturing environment needed for your spiritual growth and safe delivery into His kingdom. But an ongoing condition exists: God asks you *not to hinder His work* in the lives of you and your child.

If something—*anything*—has kept you from Christ's love, ask God to show you what it is and what you're to do about it. This could mean confessing an unloving action, attitude, or choice. It might mean forgiving another person—even one who's hurt you badly. It may simply mean accepting God's gift of life as you bring your needs—and your soon-to-be-born baby—to Him each day in prayer.

Prayer: Dear God, I don't want my thoughts, activities, or behavior to keep me or my child from coming to You. Help me, Lord! In Jesus' name, forgive me for anything I've done to hinder Your love in my family.

Journey with God: In the journaling space provided below, write down whatever God brings to your mind that will help you and your soon-to-arrive child come to Him. Let nothing hinder your praise of God or your prayers for your baby.

_____

_____

_____

_____

_____

_____

_____

_____

_____

_____

And so it was, that, while they were there, the days were accomplished that she should be delivered.

Luke 2:6, KJV

This is it! Are you ready? Do you have a bag packed, a working car with windshield wipers, gas, and keys, and some sense of direction toward the airport?

The hospital would be a better place to head, but, most likely, you'll be flying! So slow down! Take a deep breath, and inhale, "Lord, have mercy." Exhale, "Christ have mercy." Inhale prayer. Exhale worry. In, out, in, out. . . .

In this expectant moment, few people need to rush! First babies have been known to arrive in planes, trains, cabs, or cars; but most have their own timetable with lots of room for delay. That doesn't mean you can dawdle or be distracted by a sudden urge to sample prunes with pickles! You might just want to mosey on down to the hospital.

As birth pangs begin, some women experience a warm band radiating from the back of the waist. Others don't notice any signals until ripples in the front abdomen build momentum, and the push is on! The water sac breaks. Womb walls close in, and surrounding muscles press down and contract. Having lost a formerly cushy environment, the baby instinctively heads for the nearest exit!

That's your clue—not to panic but to move toward the nearest medical facility your doctor recommended. Even if

First Days of Parenting

your baby just takes his or her sweet time, you'll want the assurance of being where you need to be when these expectant days have been accomplished. The remaining work might be laborious. Yet you'll be safely delivered—right on time—into the Lord God's most highly capable and productive hands.

Prayer: Lord, have mercy! Christ, have mercy! Please guide the medical staff, and give them mercy too! Thank You for blessing me and my child with the safe delivery of Your Holy Spirit, born through the accomplishment of Jesus Christ.

Journey with God: In this space, deliver to God your concerns about labor, childbirth, or adoption procedures.

_____

_____

_____

_____

_____

_____

_____

_____

_____

_____

*I will praise thee;
for I am fearfully
and wonderfully made:
marvelous are thy works;
and that my soul knoweth right well.*

Psalm 139:14, KJV

For some reason, God made men to be fathers and women to be mothers; but, in this last stage of pregnancy, both groups sometimes feel like changing places!

"I wish I could do this for you, Honey."

"Yeah, I wish you could too!"

If you're a standby kind of guy, you might feel fifth-wheelish around a labor room. Your entire existence may seem reduced to a patting hand or a voice instructing, "Breathe!" And yet your cool head and warm presence help the soon-to-be-born mother and child more than you might guess. As you labor to become a father—or an adopting parent—you're the most likely person to pray!

So, how do you feel? Tense? Worried? Scared? Talk to God about that. Excited? Tell Him! Uncertain about handling this big responsibility? Don't keep it to yourself! Wishing you'd never been born? Stop! Don't just pray! Praise God!

Thank God that you're fearfully and wonderfully made. Thank Him for His marvelous work in creating you and giving you the joy of participating in creation through your baby's birth. Thank Him for your parents or in-laws to whom you've given the newborn role of great-grandparenting or grandparenting. Thank Him for a skilled staff of nurses, doctors, and technicians. Thank Him for pain medication as needed!

Whether you're in the labor room or somewhere outside, waiting, God brought you into this world; and He's about to do the same for your child! So let Him wait and labor with you as you pray. You can do it! Breathe deeply of His Spirit—His right and Holy Spirit—whom you can know quite well.

Prayer: Lord, help me to remember what I know! I can hardly think right now, so please remind me that You're here in Jesus' name.

Journey with God: Write down the prayers that come to you while you're waiting for your baby's arrival. Include everything for which you're thankful.

_____

_____

_____

_____

_____

_____

_____

_____

*My frame was not hidden from you,
when I was being made in secret,
intricately woven in the depths
of the earth.*

Psalm 139:15, NRSV

It's a boy! It's a girl! *It's something!* Even if you had previous tests or special requests, the lab technician or adoption agency might not have verified your baby's gender. Sometimes it's hard to say. Sometimes they don't want to risk being wrong. Sometimes expectant parents prefer not to know. But from the moment of conception, God knew! So the wondrous announcement—girl or boy—comes as no surprise to Him.

Does it to you? Hopefully you're not disappointed, but, if you are, don't lie! Talk with God about it. Tell Him—rather than family members—how you feel. Pray through your emotions instead of releasing them into a regrettable scene!

Especially, listen to God's word to you about this child. Most likely, you won't hear a booming voice over the hospital loudspeaker, but you might have a clear impression or an insightful thought that you'd never before considered. Quite possibly this word from God will reveal the secrets you have hidden from yourself, but not from Him.

For example, He may help you to remember someone's displeasure in learning you weren't a boy or girl. Or, maybe He will reveal your tendency to think life is easier for the opposite sex. (It isn't!) Or, He might show you how you'd really hoped to have a little clone of yourself—one who, of course, would lack your personal flaws!

As you talk with God, honestly and prayerfully, ask Him to remove any trace of disappointment and help you to welcome your baby with His forgiveness, acceptance, and joy. From the first moment of greeting, let your love for this child be no secret to God or anyone!

Prayer: Heavenly Father, You knew my baby's weight, length, and gender before I did! Nothing stays hidden from You! I can't hide my feelings either, Lord, so please give me Your perfect delight in this very child in Jesus' name.

Journey with God: God knew all about your baby's size, sex, and frame; but He also knows your parenting framework that's still to be seen! Ask Him to help you take note here of His love for you and your family as intricately woven in Christ.

_____

_____

_____

_____

_____

_____

_____

> *Thine eyes did see my substance,*
> *yet being unperfect;*
> *and in thy book*
> *all my members were written,*
> *which in continuance*
> *were fashioned, when as yet there*
> *was none of them.*
>
> Psalm 139:16, KJV

What a beautiful baby! As soon as you're given your freshly wrapped bundle, you'll notice that precious rosebud mouth. You'll stroke the downy head with its first fuzz of hair and kiss those wrinkled-silk cheeks. When you've counted all the toes and fingers, you'll put your own finger in the tiny palm to check the baby's grip, and you'll feel oddly pleased—and awed.

What a precious baby! If you had to overcome any complications before your arrival at this moment, you'll probably feel like laughing and crying at the same time! Your eyes will widen with wonder as feathery lashes flutter and eyelids open, big, to their very first sight of you.

What a perfect baby! Even if this tiny person has an obvious flaw, you can still be assured of perfection simply because your son or daughter has achieved a purpose in being born. Life, death, and defective human standards cannot take away the perfection which has now come in the completion of God's unique design.

What a wonderful baby! Throughout your child's life, God will continuously fashion him or her into the shape and substance He most wants this person to be. Thank Him for the privilege of being part of this marvelous growth.

Thank Him for your own perfection, found only in your perfect Savior, Jesus Christ.

Prayer: Heavenly Father, praise You for Your holiness. Praise You for giving birth to Your perfect Son, Jesus, who came to save me from imperfection and restore me to life in Your Holy Spirit in His name. Praise You for the birth of my child!

Journey with God: Use this journaling space to record the wonders you feel about your baby—thoughts you'll want to remember and share in years to come.

_____

_____

_____

_____

_____

_____

_____

_____

_____

_____

_____

_____

In your book were written all the days that were formed for me, when none of them as yet existed.

Psalm 139:16, NRSV

From the very first moment you hold your baby, you'll probably wonder: *Am I doing this right?* New fathers often admit to feeling clumsy or fearful about how they're to handle an infant, but new mothers seldom feel too sure of themselves either!

Confidence builds with practice of parenting skills. To help you get started, the hospital or adoption agency can have someone show you a safe position for holding a newborn. A pediatric nurse might schedule a brief class, right there in the maternity ward. Or the pediatrician might come by to give you some leaflets and answer questions.

At this stage of parenting, the information most needed concerns basic skills of a physical nature. For example, you need to know a safe, comfortable way to hold, feed, clean, and cover your infant. You need to know how to support the head and lower back until your child can do that solo. You need to know how to protect the baby's umbilical cord, bring up those air bubbles that cause tummy aches, and put on a diaper that won't immediately fall off!

If you've never been around infants—or if you've had a past miscarriage or a present medical alert—you might feel especially fearful about the future well-being of this child.

That's perfectly normal and also understandable. However, you need to understand that God, not you, is the real parent! He ordains your baby's days—and your days of parenting too. So He knows *what you need* to take care of the little one He has entrusted to you. Let Him hold you. Trust Him to do it right.

Prayer: Heavenly Father, I'm so afraid I'll do something wrong! Please help me to relax in Jesus' name.

Journey with God: List characteristics of God—Father, Son, and Holy Spirit—that make Him perfectly suited to parenting you and your new family well!

_____

_____

_____

_____

_____

_____

_____

_____

_____

_____

_____

Day 9

While he [Jesus] was saying this, a woman in the crowd raised her voice and said to him, "Blessed is the womb that bore you and the breasts that nursed you!" But he said, "Blessed rather are those who hear the word of God and obey it!"

Luke 11:27–28, NRSV

Nothing compares with childbirth! In this wondrous event—blessed by God since the beginning of creation—a unique, remarkable human being has struggled to be born!

If you're the biological parents, you've shared the pleasure and the pain—both of which continue somewhat after the delivery. Assuming everything went well, you'll feel a pleasant sense of relief—even euphoria. But, for a few days, you and baby may be tired from the strenuous workout!

If you're the new mother, you may have some additional discomfort as your body readapts. This is to be expected as organs return to the positions they had before a baby began to rearrange them! With tension released, the womb readjusts to a natural state, lessening the possibility of hemorrhage.

Most doctors agree that breast-feeding helps the womb contract with greater ease and speed. This helps the infant, too, since the mother's milk contains protective nutrients not found anywhere else. The baby will also be less likely to have an allergic reaction but more likely to develop a close attachment to the mother.

First Days of Parenting

Giving birth and nursing a child just naturally bring a wondrous blessing! But, hearing and obeying God's Word brings a greater *supernatural* blessing to all people—fathers, mothers, and biological or adopted children—born to God through the grace and benediction of the Lord Jesus Christ.

Prayer: Heavenly Father, thank You for the wonder of birth. Thank You for bearing with us in bringing Your Word into the world in Jesus' name.

Journey with God: Ask God to help you recognize natural and supernatural blessings accompanying the birth of your child.

_____

_____

_____

_____

_____

_____

_____

_____

_____

_____

After eight days had passed, it was time to circumcise the child, and he was called Jesus.

Luke 2:21, NRSV

Before you bring home a newborn son, you have to decide whether to give the medical clinic or hospital permission for your baby's circumcision. If you have a new daughter, you may think, "Thank God! That's one decision I don't have to make!" True, but the matter still affects your family.

Any parent of any child needs information about medical facts which might eventually concern them. For instance, you may want to ask your doctor about studies showing that women married to circumcised men are less likely to have cervical cancer. Or you may be interested in knowing more about the ease of cleanliness for a circumcised male.

One very interesting fact you might ask about concerns blood clotting. Research indicates that the body's ability to clot the blood safely isn't found at birth but by the end of the first week. Since the Jewish rite of circumcision, which began a few thousand years ago, occurs on the eighth day, who but God would have known about this "recent" discovery!

The procedure didn't begin with infants, though. It started as a sign of God's covenant with Abraham, a grown man. Later, the time came during puberty or just prior to marriage. But, regardless of the male's age, God initiated this sign to mark His chosen people. In the light of Christ, it has even more significance: Himself circumcised, Jesus became the holy Bridegroom for His bride, the Church. Boy or girl, that includes your baby—and you!

Prayer: Dear God, circumcision seems like a strange choice for making a pact with You! I understand better when the Bible talks about circumcising the heart. Help me to have this internal sign of Your covenant in Christ's name.

Journey with God: Have you been closed off or unresponsive to God in some area of your life? Ask Him to help you know in your heart how to prepare yourself and family to receive Him.

___

___

___

___

___

___

___

___

___

> *And she gave birth to her firstborn, a son. She wrapped him in cloths and placed him in a manger, because there was no room for them in the inn.*
>
> Luke 2:7, NIV

Do you have a room ready for your baby? Does it have a crib mobile waiting for a tiny hand to bat butterflies or to make little animals spin and dance? Do fluffy lambs, bears, or bunnies prance along the gaily colored border of a freshly papered wall?

If you're like many first-time parents, you've spent a great deal of time, thought, and, maybe, money decorating the nursery. You've discovered family heirlooms and perhaps found treasures, such as a rocking horse, a homemade toy box, or an antique cradle that you've recently refinished.

If cost wasn't a concern, you might have bought a brand new, beautifully coordinated crib set. But, even if you could not afford anything fancy, you did what you could to create a safe, pleasant environment for your child. Maybe that meant regluing wicker on an old bassinet you found in a secondhand furniture store then spray-painting—with lead-free paint, of course! But, somehow, you prepared a place for your child.

Mary and Joseph did too. Although they had no decorative nursery with animals painted around, they did have a softly braying donkey or real-live lamb hovering over their Son. The manger where He lay truly was a *crib*—a feedbox for animals! Yet, with these barest of essentials, Jesus' parents arranged a safe and pleasant place for their Child. As you do what you can to provide essentials for your baby, begin by simply *making room*: Make room in your life for your family. Make room in your family for God's Son.

Prayer: Heavenly Father, forgive me for worrying about money, time, or space instead of giving first place to You! Please fill our child's room and our home with Your Holy Presence in Christ's name.

Journey with God: Ask God to bring to your mind anything He considers essential that's lacking in your home or nursery.

_____

_____

_____

_____

_____

_____

_____

_____

_____

_____

He shall feed his flock like a shepherd: he shall gather the lambs with his arm, and carry them in his bosom, and shall gently lead those that are with young.

Isaiah 40:11, KJV

Before you transport your baby home from the hospital or adoption agency, investigate the legal requirements in your state. Most likely, you'll have to place an approved infant carrier in the backseat of a car. Since these can be costly, you might ask about borrowing or renting one for awhile. Or, see if the medical or adoption facility has a state-approved infant seat they'll loan you just to get your baby home.

When you're ready to buy a car carrier, look for one your child can use as long as required. Such equipment often surpasses safety codes and can adjust to your child's rapidly changing size and individual needs. For instance, if the seat fits on a kitchen countertop, you can place your baby in it at mealtime when he or she has advanced to a menu of strained food. Or you might set it in a shopping cart to protect your infant from tumbling—or from being too close to other people's hands!

At home, though, your baby will prefer the close contact of being carried. You will, too, unless your arms grow weary, and then a sling, supported by your back and shoulders, might work well. Either way, your baby will rest against your chest and listen to the soothing beat of your

First Days of Parenting

heart. This healthy touch helps to nurture and comfort your baby—and you! Right now, you may need some comfort as you take your infant home. You may wonder how on earth you can do what's needed to take care of this child, and by yourself you can't! But God the Father *gently leads* parents with young children. He holds and comforts you. He carries you next to His heart.

Prayer: Heavenly Father, thank You for carrying me as I carry my child home! Thank You for leading me in Jesus' name.

Journey with God: Talk with God about your fears in coming home with your new baby.

Day 13

Like someone who heats and purifies silver, he will purify the Levites and make them pure like gold and silver. Then they will bring offerings to the LORD in the right way.

Malachi 3:3, NCV

As you bring your newborn home from the hospital, one of your first concerns will be having everything clean and ready to welcome your child. Even if the furnishings aren't brand new, you've hopefully had a chance to disinfect the surfaces in the nursery. If not, concentrate on areas with which the baby will come in contact.

For other helps with sanitation, your obstetrician or hospital has probably given you some sanitizing wipes to use before you nurse your child. If your baby will be formula-fed, you might have received a supply of pre-mixed bottles. These lessen the chore of sterilizing nipples and preparing formula during the first few days home. Later, you can cut expenses by preparing formula from canned or powdered milk.

If you have a dishwasher, its intense heat should be adequate for sterilizing baby bottles. Most dishwashers also have a small, enclosed basket that's great for bottle rings and nipples which, otherwise, gravitate toward the heating element and promptly melt! A microwave sanitizes bottles too, if you have a container for that purpose. Or you can set a bottle rack in boiling water on a stove for several minutes.

First Days of Parenting

This is your baby! Naturally, you want to do everything the right way. However, you do have choices about how you'll sterilize formula and equipment. So, choose what works best for you, using God's Word as your guide: Let heat and water purge the dross from each leftover bottle and purify whatever goes into your baby's mouth!

Prayer: Dear Lord, thank You for always practicing what You teach! Thank You for purifying my family in Jesus' name.

Journey with God: Jot down questions you have about sanitary conditions for your family. For general answers, look in the Book of Leviticus. For specific concerns, ask God to bring to your mind His pure view of this subject.

_____

_____

_____

_____

_____

_____

_____

_____

_____

And all they that heard them laid them up in their hearts, saying, What manner of child shall this be! And the hand of the Lord was with him.

Luke 1:66, KJV

Can you tell yet who the baby looks like? Many parents think they can! "Hey! He's got your eyes!" Or, "Look at her long fingers—just like mine!" If you've adopted a child or infant, you might even check your family photo album and find an uncanny resemblance to someone, including yourself at that age. After all, this is your child!

Every parent wants to see who the baby looks like, but a danger comes in comparing unfavorably, or feeling left out. "Don't you think she looks anything like me?"—a question usually meaning, "Don't you love me anymore?" Or, "Yep, he's the spitting image of his father"—a phrase often reserved for those unflattering moments when baby spits up or drools!

As you look for resemblances, include both sides of the family since your baby comes with two sets of parentage. Be especially aware of sensitivities so you can avoid remarks such as, "Oh, no! Our precious baby has your family's floppy ears!" Even if your child or other relatives never know what you've said, the connecting parent does!

From the moment of conception, your baby inherits these physical characteristics, but more important is the heritage that your attitudes bring. From the very start, you can't

First Days of Parenting

do much to change features or coloring, but you can lay to heart your decision to act in a loving manner toward your baby and each other. The hand of the Lord is with you! Therefore, you can place His value, not on physical appearances, but on what manner of child this will be.

Prayer: Dear God, please help our family look like You in Jesus' name!

Journey with God: What resemblance to Christ do you bear as a Christian? Ask God to show you what manner of child He wants you to be.

_____

_____

_____

_____

_____

_____

_____

_____

_____

_____

> *This will be a sign for you: you will find a child wrapped in bands of cloth and lying in a manger.*
>
> Luke 2:12, NRSV

Today's babies usually wear "bands" of plastic, not cloth! Plastic-coated, disposable diapers fit children of every size—from premature infants to hefty toddlers ready for training pants. A plastic band, fastened on a tiny wrist soon after birth, helps the hospital identify your newborn— who might also have a plastic-wrapped tummy!

Cloth, paper, or plastic, these bands share the purpose of protecting your infant, but they're also a sign of your child's dependence on you. For example, the umbilical cord— which once nurtured the embryo, fetus, and unborn infant— has now been cut, cleaned, and protectively covered. Yet it visually reminds you of how completely your infant depends on you for proper nourishment and care.

If you're uncertain what to do to tend that vulnerable area, a pediatrician or nurse can show you how to keep it dry and sanitized for a few days. Then presto! The umbilical cord disappears into a cute little tummy button—a sign of those fun days of playing yet to come!

Meanwhile, *let this be a sign to you of your dependence on God.* You'll never outgrow your need for Him, no matter how skilled you become as a parent or how mature as a Christian. If you ever think you've "made it" or developed so well you don't need God, something inside your soul or spirit will dry up and shrivel as surely as your baby's umbilical cord is doing now. So just plan to stay dependent on God—forever!

Prayer: Lord, I've heard the world say, "God helps those who help themselves," but now I see that's a lie! Thank You for letting me know *You help those who depend on You*. I need You, and my family needs You. Please keep us wrapped in Your Holy Spirit and safely bound in Jesus' name.

Journey with God: Note the ways your baby obviously depends on you. Ask God about your less obvious dependence on Him.

_____

_____

_____

_____

_____

_____

_____

_____

Day 16

He said, "You must obey the LORD your God and do what he says is right. If you obey all his commands and keep his rules, I will not bring on you any of the sicknesses I brought on the Egyptians. I am the LORD who heals you."

Exodus 15:26, NCV

Most new parents feel plagued with worries about germs! They hesitate to have a newborn around family and friends who might suffocate their baby with kisses, breathe all over the poor child's face, or grab their precious bundle with unwashed hands! Since your job as a parent does include protection, you need to decide what you want to do about visitors—and their behavior!

For instance, you may need to say, "You're welcome to hold the baby just as soon as you've washed your hands." Or, "Please kiss the forehead, but not the mouth." If you suspect that someone might be offended by such statements—or if you question their state of health—avoid unnecessary strain on you and your child by staying away from that person for now.

Premature infants or children with any type of medical concern usually need to be isolated from the general public. In grocery stores, for example, total strangers sometimes come up and pinch little cheeks as though they're inspecting fresh fruit! (The baby doesn't care, but you might!)

Most people who want to see your child will respect your requests. But, even if you can't avoid contact with germs, don't be plagued! Illnesses may arrive in a specific

First Days of Parenting

season for a specific reason, but in God's will come health and hope and healing. Ask Him to protect your child—and you!

Prayer: Heavenly Father, thank You for the blessed well-being that comes only from You. I want to do what I can to prevent the spread of disease in my family—not just physically, but also the disease that comes from being out of line with Your will. Help me to be at ease with You in Jesus' name.

Journey with God: Discuss with God any concerns you have about your child's health or your own.

_____

_____

_____

_____

_____

_____

_____

_____

_____

_____

Day 17

And the girl went and got the baby's mother. Pharaoh's daughter said to her, "Take this baby and nurse him for me, and I will pay you." So the woman took the baby and nursed him.

Exodus 2:8b-9, NIV

When you were growing up in church or parochial school, did you ever hear the story of baby Moses? Did you wonder why he turned from his royal Egyptian upbringing to lead the Hebrew people out of captivity into a binding relationship with God? Did you guess it all started with early bonding?

From the very start, the Lord had His hand on Moses. He put the right people in the right place at the right time to provide for the infant's care. Then as Moses became an adult, God continued to give him the right background and experience to do the job he'd been called to do.

As God led this future leader's upbringing, He thought of every detail. He knew, for example, that the first hours, days, and weeks of a baby's life offer the optimum bonding time for a strong future relationship. So, He arranged for the biological mother to nurse and tend the child—which gave close contact with Dad and other family members too!

In these first days of parenting, your family can also enjoy a time of bonding. Even if you're not thrilled to lose the sleep, you can rejoice—night and day—in the blessed opportunities God gives you to hold, rock, and comfort your child. Biological or adopted, your family will gain strength by being in the right place at the right time for snuggling! Your loving attachment to one another will grow—naturally and supernaturally—as you spend blessed time together, firmly bound by God's love.

Prayer: Holy Father, thank You for the bond You're creating between me and my child. Help us to be well-bonded to You in Jesus' name.

Journey with God: Is fear from your past days of childhood, your present lack of experience, or your concerns about the future preventing you from creating a strong bond with your child? Give each fear to God, and listen for His word to you.

_____

_____

_____

_____

_____

_____

_____

_____

_____

_____

> *Children's children are
> a crown to the aged,
> and parents are the pride
> of their children.*
>
> Proverbs 17:6, NIV

Have your parents seen the baby yet? In the first few days at home, you may want to limit visitors to your closest friends and relatives who are eager to welcome your child. This especially includes the baby's great-grandparents or grandparents who probably can't wait to see and hold your little one!

Unless a doctor advised your family not to have callers, these first days of greeting your child help special people in your life create an even stronger bond with your family. However, if you've often felt like severing ties, you may be even more tempted to do so now!

That's up to you—and God. So talk with Him about your pain, hurt, or annoyance concerning any close relative to whom you don't feel close at all! Ask Him to give you His view of old squabbles, including wounded pride. Ask for His understanding of the other person's point of view. Ask Him to clarify your perception of love and respect regarding that person. Ask Him to help you forgive—and to be forgiven too.

If the relationship involves severe or ongoing wounds, you certainly don't need that added strain! So, be open to God's leading. He may give you the impression that you're to avoid contact, or He may let you know it's time for healing. Perhaps He'll bring to your mind the importance of letting this person help you with the baby or handle physical tasks, such as vacuuming or cooking meals or running errands.

In God's perfect order, each generation will respect and value the other. Each will see the good, the love, the caring that's intended. If that hasn't happened in your family, just remember: Only God can wholly heal and restore. Only He can perfect His perfect order for your family.

Prayer: Lord, I want so much for my family to be proud of me! I want their love too—not just for myself but for the new family You've given me with the coming of this child. Help me to trust You to bring what's needed in Your perfect time and place in Jesus' name.

Journey with God: Talk with God about your family. Listen for the response He writes on your heart or mind.

_____

_____

_____

_____

_____

_____

_____

Day 19

> *Guided by the Spirit,
> Simeon came into the temple;
> and when the parents brought in the
> child Jesus, to do for him what was
> customary under the law,
> Simeon took him in his arms
> and praised God.*
>
> Luke 2:27–28, NRSV

As bonding occurs in your family, you can draw Christian ties together too. From the moment Abraham offered his long-awaited son Isaac, parents with a Judeo-Christian background have given their children as a *living* sacrifice to God. How you go about this will depend, of course, on your church's customs or what you're personally impressed by God to do.

For instance, some churches have a dedication service for young children, which might be scheduled on Mother's Day. In denominations encouraging infant baptism, a service can be arranged for almost any Sunday or other day that's convenient for the minister or priest and the parents or other family members who want to attend. Either occasion has the purpose of committing yourselves to this new child and to raising him or her with God's guidance.

If you've recently given birth, your pastor may have visited you in the hospital and perhaps talked with you about a dedication or baptismal service. If not, you may want to set up an appointment to ask questions, discuss a time, and make any other arrangements needed for this important event.

The idea is to present your child to God and receive His blessing through your acceptance of the Lord Jesus Christ and His Church. Although the ceremony itself will vary from one denomination to another, each involves a commitment from you as the parent. This means you'll be asked to make a pledge, promise, or vow, stating that you will do what you can to bring up your child in a manner that's pleasing to God.

Prayer: Heavenly Father, I want to be the kind of parent You want for my child, but I can't do that without You! I need Your help, Your power, Your blessing, and the support of Your Church in Jesus' name.

Journey with God: Ask God to bring to your mind His thoughts about committing your child's life and your parenting years to Him.

_____

_____

_____

_____

_____

_____

_____

_____

Day 20

I [God] put beautiful clothes made with needlework on you and put sandals of fine leather on your feet. I wrapped you in fine linen and covered you with silk.

Ezekiel 16:10, NCV

If you've arranged for a dedication or baptismal service at your church, you've given a lot of thought to what your baby will wear. Maybe you still have the baptismal gown you wore as an infant. Or, perhaps a grandparent has embroidered a beautiful outfit just for the dedication ceremony.

Although the actual service may last less than an hour, your baby still needs to be comfortable in a soft fabric, such as silk, that doesn't pinch or rub tender skin. For your baby's everyday wearing apparel, you'll want to select soft clothing, too—but probably not silk!

Soft cotton knits provide a practical wardrobe for your infant. Not only are they easy for you to launder, they'll feel good against your baby's skin—assuming the washing machine gets all the suds out! If not, just add less soap and more water to take out that scratchy feeling. Soft fabrics soothe and protect your baby's delicate skin. So does looseness in the cut and style of clothing. And these practical outfits also help you. Instead of struggling to squeeze little arms and legs through tight and tiny holes, you'll be able to slide your baby easily into loose garments without upset-

First Days of Parenting

ting either of you! Drawstrings, snaps, and Velcro help you dress a squirming infant too.

As you provide sensible clothing for your baby, thank God for the wondrous covering He's put on you! In the pattern and power of His Son, Jesus, He's clothed you with beautiful, fine fabric and presented you, glorious, unto Himself.

Prayer: Heavenly Father, thank You for Your provisions for me and my family in Jesus' name.

Journey with God: Do you look incredibly handsome or simply beautiful? You are! Ask God to help you see yourself as He sees you—His lovely, precious child.

_____

_____

_____

_____

_____

_____

_____

_____

_____

_____

_____

*When they saw this,
they made known what had been
told them about this child.*

Luke 2:17, NRSV

Have you had a chance to send out announcements of your child's birth or adoption? Many hospitals provide the local newspaper with a list of infants born each week, giving the date, baby's name, and names of the parents. Some papers will publish additional information about your child or a small photograph that you supply.

Announcements to the general public will notify people who sell baby products, too, so expect mail or telephone solicitations. However, the newspaper spreads your good news to neighbors, acquaintances, or others in your community whom you haven't yet had a chance to notify. Also, you might want to call the church office if a notice doesn't automatically appear in the weekly bulletin or monthly newsletter.

Most parents send announcements to friends and relatives in other cities too. In the greeting card section of almost any store, you'll find a wide selection of messages and card designs to announce your baby's arrival. Angels and a bright star announced the birth of Baby Jesus. Prophets published messages of His coming, centuries before He arrived. The Gospels and Revelation tell of His return. But

First Days of Parenting

people who visited the Holy Child in person made known to His parents the awesome wonders they had seen.

As people come to see your baby, someone may announce a God-given message to you! "This is a special child," or, "What a sweet spirit your baby has!" By accepting such a word with prayer and thanksgiving, you may come to hear what God announces to you about your child!

Prayer: Heavenly Father, I keep thinking our baby is ours, but I'm coming to see that You're already at work in this new life in Jesus' name. Thank You!

Journey with God: Ask God to announce what He wants you to come to see or hear about your child.

_____

_____

_____

_____

_____

_____

_____

_____

_____

_____

_____

> *When it was time for Elizabeth to give birth, she had a boy. Her neighbors and relatives heard how good the Lord was to her, and they rejoiced with her.*
>
> Luke 1:57–58, NCV

What makes you so special? What indication do you have that your son or daughter comes to you as an extraordinary gift from God? What would your family like for other people to know so they, too, will rejoice in the wondrous, blessed arrival of your child?

As you fill in the blanks on the birth or adoption announcement you've chosen, you'll probably have spaces to tell about your baby's name, weight, length, birthdate, or age. As you complete this information, ask God to help you fill in blanks about the good news He's given you to proclaim to your church, relatives, and friends.

For example, were you once told that you'd never have children but now you do? Did God see you through a difficult pregnancy or labor? Did He bring you a daughter even though you came from a family of ten sons? Did you have concerns about the child's health or availability for adoption, but somehow everything worked out fine? In the good news about your son or daughter, do you have any good news to share?

Think about it. Pray about it. Ask God to bring to your attention any blessings you've discovered in your new family. Surely you do not—even for a moment—think, "Aw, it's just another kid!" Something truly wondrous has happened—the miracle of life has visited your home! So, tell others about God's hand in the arrival of your child. Announce to everyone that He is what's special in your lives!

Prayer: Dear God, You really are good to us! Thank You so much for our little one, borne by Your Spirit in Jesus' name.

Journey with God: In your journaling space, write down every God-timed thought or moment you want to remember about the coming of your child. Share this good news with others.

_____

_____

_____

_____

_____

_____

_____

_____

_____

_____

_____

> *But Mary kept all these things,*
> *and pondered them in her heart.*
>
> Luke 2:19, KJV

Before you forget the good news and wondrous events that preceded or immediately followed your child's arrival, write them down. A baby book provides a good place for keeping new information, "first" facts, and snapshots of your child.

In most baby books, you'll find pages for keeping track of first-time experiences. For instance, you can record the gifts your child received at birth, adoption, or during your first holidays together. You can note growth increases and log in visits to the pediatrician with the date and type of shots received. In days to come, you can jot down favorites, such as toys, songs, games, or bedtime stories.

Most likely, you'll want to keep track of more than just vital statistics. After all, this is your son's or daughter's history (or her-story) in the making! So find pages in the baby book where you can write down your thoughts and feelings as you watch your little one grow.

For example, how did you feel when you learned you'd be a parent? What hopes, plans, or goals did you have? What prayers? What did it cost for a carton of milk, a movie, or the place where your family lived? What happened at home, at work, in the local community, or in the world on

First Days of Parenting

the day your daughter or son arrived? What went through your head as you saw your child for the first time? What did you say? What do you want to keep, recall, and treasure always?

As you ponder these things in your heart, record them with thanks to God. Write down each prayer and blessing you'd like to remember. Someday your child will want to hear all about these special days—your very first days of parenting!

Prayer: Father, help me to see, keep, and treasure what You want at the heart of this family in Christ's name.

Journey with God: Listen to God's personal word to you about your child as He brings impressions to your mind or an inner awareness to your spirit. Record those thoughts here.

_____

_____

_____

_____

_____

_____

_____

_____

_____

> *Bless the LORD, O my soul:*
> *and all that is within me,*
> *bless his holy name.*
>
> Psalm 103:1, KJV

Not long after the news about your child goes out, you will probably receive cards and gifts from family, friends, coworkers, or members of your church. Letters may even arrive from people you haven't heard from for awhile, and each response will have special significance to you.

For example, an estranged friend might use this occasion to let you know you're remembered fondly. A distant relative who's been through a similar experience might become closer or ask to keep in touch. An employer may let you know your work has been more appreciated than you suspected! A sibling with whom you often bicker may use your child's arrival as an excuse to call or drop by more often for a pleasant chat.

As these gifts come, express your thanks to the persons involved—and to God. Although you'll probably reserve your thank-you notes for gift-wrapped presents, acknowledge each gift of thoughtfulness. Make a point of ending each telephone call or visit on a note of gratitude.

At times when you're not thankful for a thoughtless word or act toward your family, be quick to forgive! Be generous toward those who seem to criticize your developing skills as a parent. Ask God to heal any hurts they've caused, but also be careful not to chastise yourself harshly! You're learning! You're beginning to discover something new each day about your child and your ability to care for him or her. So, let nothing hinder that joy, that blessing. Let all that is within you be right with God and thankful to Him as you bless His holy name.

Prayer: O, Lord, I am thankful for You, my family, and the kindness of others. But sometimes a careless remark makes me feel so small! Help me to be quick to confess any attitudes that hinder me from fully blessing Jesus' name.

Journey with God: Does all that is within you and your family bless the name of the Lord? Discuss this with God.

_____

_____

_____

_____

_____

_____

_____

_____

_____

_____

*Bless the LORD, O my soul,
and forget not all his benefits.*
Psalm 103:2, KJV

Read any good books lately? Had any good sleep? Or, have you had it with those all-night marathons that you're afraid will last until your child turns thirty-one? (Then, you might be asked to baby-sit your infant grandchildren!)

Right now, you certainly have not forgotten the benefit of sleep, but you may have forgotten to rest when you had the chance. For example, you might have been able to cut short a phone call while your little one slept. If so, consider using an answering machine when you need a quiet time. Or, maybe a nap will cut into a prime-time television show you hate to miss, but, hey, that means you can thank God for reruns or VCRs!

As you take care of your child—especially during those wee hours when a wee one interrupts your sleep—forget not the benefit of resting when you can. Forget not the benefit of resting in the Lord.

For example, as you rock your child in the middle of the night, softly sing your favorite hymns or recite the Twenty-third Psalm. As you feed your baby, pray. Talk with God about your concerns and your delights in this child. Thank Him for His help. Claim Bible promises for each family member. Speak words of comfort, rest, and healing in Christ's name.

In your prayers, include a time of praise. List every benefit you can think of that comes to you simply because you know God. Praise Him as your Father and Creator. Praise Him as God's Son and your personal Savior. Praise Him as Holy Spirit, alive in you and your family. Praise Him as Provider of all good, including a good night—or good day—of rest!

Prayer: Dear Lord, I'm so tired! Sometimes I think I'll never have a whole night's sleep, but You know better! Help me to trust You for all that my family and I need in Jesus' name.

Journey with God: Write down the benefits of knowing God that He brings to your mind—thoughts that help you rest in Him.

_____

_____

_____

_____

_____

_____

_____

_____

Day 26

*Wash me thoroughly
from mine iniquity,
and cleanse me from my sin.*

Psalm 51:2, KJV

If your first days of parenting involve a newborn, your doctor may have suggested you sponge-bathe your baby until the umbilical cord has healed. When that occurs, you may feel hesitant to plunge into a full bath-time, but, once you do, you and your baby will probably enjoy the regular routine.

At first, you both might feel nervous or scared. To lessen tension, dive into a daily schedule at a time of day or evening when neither of you feels fretful or fussy! For some people, that's early morning; for others, late evening. Either way, alternate the time as needed to see what works best. A lively morning bath can help you both wake up. A quiet evening bath can lull your child before bedtime.

Until your baby can sit up steadily without toppling, a plastic tub on a kitchen counter works well. This allows you to be closer to your child, stand without too much bending, and have easy access to the faucet and sink drain as you fill or dump the water from the tub.

To get into a comfortable, safe position, cradle your infant in the arm you use least often. Then lower both your arm and your baby into a half-filled tub of pleasantly warm water. This frees the hand you use the most to soap and rinse with greater dexterity—and more confidence too!

As you wash little body parts, let God's peace wash over you. Talk to Him and your baby in low, crooning tones. If you would rather sing softly, by all means do! Trust your God-given instincts! Make bath-time a happy time—a fret-free cleansing time—with your baby and your Lord.

Prayer: Dear Father, please wash away anything that mars my mind or spirit and my pleasure in this child. Thank You for cleansing me with Your Spirit in the power of Jesus' name.

Journey with God: Is an attitude or action blemishing your family? Ask God to help you see any soiled spots you might have overlooked so you can offer them to Him for cleansing.

___

___

___

___

___

___

___

___

> *Cleanse me with hyssop,
> and I will be clean; wash me,
> and I will be whiter than snow.*
>
> Psalm 51:7, NIV

Clean babies have the nicest smell! When they don't, that's usually a signal that a diaper needs changing or an upset tummy needs comforting. But, even under those conditions, a breast-fed infant seldom has an objectionable odor. This is great for parents or visitors holding the baby! Yet other senses need to stay alert to such a child.

In the first days of infancy, babies don't care if they have chubby cheeks free of lipstick or a fresh outfit with matching socks! They won't complain about such matters. What will bother them, though, is having wet, soiled clothes or diapers that chafe their tender skin. Silky little bottoms and skin-folds behind the ears or beneath the arms and chin seem most apt to develop a rash. Then the discomfort from prickling, itching, or burning can be enough to make your baby cry! So, until your new daughter or son can say, "Yo, Ma or Pa, I have a rash," crying lets you know, "This does NOT feel good!"

To keep your baby soft and sweet smelling, you'll need to develop a sweetly-sensitive nose! This means being aware of messy diapers or spit-up that has a way of oozing beneath the chin. Also, it means avoiding fragrances that mask odors and keep you from knowing your baby needs tending. Perfumes or artificial scents often cause allergic reactions anyway!

Nothing smells as good as a clean, healthy, well-tended baby. So take a deep breath, keep plenty of plain water on hand, and bring forth your baby's perfectly natural and wondrously fresh smell!

Prayer: Dear God, why do people try to cover up what doesn't "smell right" instead of facing the problem and taking care of it? I know I do this too, but I still don't understand! Help me to discern and admit my mistakes quickly. Thank You for tending my family in the cleansing power of Jesus' name.

Journey with God: Ask God to reveal any mess you've tried to keep hidden from yourself.

*As a mother comforts her child,
so I will comfort you.*

Isaiah 66:13, NRSV

No doubt about it, upset tummies evoke sour odors and baby tears. When this happens, night after night, you might feel like crying too!

Bottle-fed newborns often need time for their stomachs to adjust; but if milk consistently disagrees with them, ask the pediatrician about changing formula. Some babies have a lactose intolerance and need a soybean or other substitute. But if no one on either side of the family dislikes the taste of milk, there's a strong probability your baby will soon digest it fine.

Some babies cry because they drink more than their tummies can handle. Others just need another gentle pat on the upper back (below the neck and between the shoulder blades) to bring up air bubbles. Most likely, though, your baby awakens at night with a tummy upset only by emptiness!

Ask a pediatrician about your baby's needs. Generally, premature babies need an ounce or two of milk every two or three hours. Full-term infants need a two to ten-ounce bottle or breast-feeding every four hours or so. Then, most babies will drink more and sleep longer as they develop more fully.

First Days of Parenting

As your child awakens at night, milk will comfort his or her empty tummy. But there's a deeper emptiness that everyone —premature baby or mature adult—continuously needs to have filled: the need for love. Feeding your baby fills a little tummy and gives loving comfort at the same time. As you rock or hold your child at any hour, let God embrace you with the comfort of His love.

Prayer: Heavenly Father, sometimes I feel so empty. Help me to receive an infilling of Your Holy Spirit—night and day—in Jesus' name.

Journey with God: Do you feel an insatiable need for love and comfort? Talk with God about this. Listen for His response.

_____

_____

_____

_____

_____

_____

_____

_____

_____

_____

Day 29

> LORD, *listen to my words.*
> *Understand my sadness.*
>
> Psalm 5:1, NCV

"I don't know what's the matter with me! Sometimes I burst into tears or get weepy for no reason."

Commonly known as "baby blues," postpartum depression often affects new mothers as they physically adjust and gain hormonal balance. Dads or adopting moms have similar symptoms from lack of sleep or concerns about parental responsibility. Yet those experiences also affect biological mothers who fret about temporary loss of energy—and shapely figures too!

If baby blues have colored your first days of parenting, you'll be glad to know they won't last forever. Meanwhile, you might try to get more rest than you'd normally require. Make sure you have well-balanced meals and natural vitamin supplements as needed. Also, lift your spirits by filling your home with the sounds of psalms and your favorite hymns.

You'll probably find that talking with an experienced, Christian parent—your own or someone else's—will help you adjust to the changes your child brings. But nothing takes the place of talking regularly with the Lord. Night or day, He's available to listen, hear, and understand everything you think or feel.

No other person can fully fathom the depth of your sadness. No one else can stay close to you around the clock to discuss every concern, large or small. No one but God can bring the comfort, rest, and healing that you need.

Prayer: Dear Heavenly Father, I feel so blue! I know this happens to other parents, but I hadn't expected it myself! There's rarely time to rest. I don't always feel like eating super-nutritiously. And I'm not thrilled about the physical changes I see! Help! Please give me the strength to take care of myself well so I can care for my family in Jesus' name.

Journey with God: Discuss with God whatever is troubling you. Listen to His word to you as you journal in the space below.

Day 30

*As a father has compassion
on his children,
so the LORD has compassion
on those who fear him.*

Psalm 103:13, NIV

"Hey! Everyone said I'd know what my baby's cries mean, but I don't have the slightest idea! Would someone please tell me—NOW?"

They probably would if they knew! From birth, most babies make sounds like any other baby, yet not quite the same. Each has a unique personality and a voice range that varies and carries according to the present mood!

Throughout the day and evening, fluctuating conditions affect your child. Tiredness, hunger, uncomfortable positions, or other irritations will make your baby cry. If this goes on too long, the wails can set off other reactions, such as an excessive intake of air from crying so hard. Then, you need to bring up air bubbles as you do during feeding time.

Compassion and common sense will let you know what your ear has not yet discovered! So trust yourself and God's leading to tell you what you need to know. Eventually, you'll discern each variation in sound and think, "Oh, that's a hungry cry." Or, "This sounds like someone's tired." Or, "I think the baby has a tummy ache."

Meanwhile, remember: Babies cry for a reason—even if you're unsure what it is! This doesn't mean you've done one single thing wrong. It just means your baby is doing right in letting you know, "There's a problem here!" So, listen very carefully, and you'll be surprised how quickly you know what the problem is. Once it's been identified, you'll soon know a logical and loving solution too.

Prayer: Dear God, thank You for Your insight into my child so I'll know just what to do. Help me to be more aware of Your compassion for me in Jesus' name.

Journey with God: Do you ever feel as though you cry for help and no one answers? Ask God to help you hear His quick and loving response to your needs.

_____

_____

_____

_____

_____

_____

_____

_____

_____

_____

_____

> *But I am calm and quiet, like a baby with its mother. I am at peace, like a baby with its mother.*
>
> Psalm 131:2, NCV

When you pick up your baby, do you get an immediate response? Does he hush right away? Does she quickly quieten as you hold her in your arms?

As babies become more aware of a parent's voice, smile, or embrace, they're apt to want only mom or dad to hold them. If someone else tries to pick them up, they may vocalize displeasure with a sudden wail or burst of tears.

In the first days of parenting, your baby probably won't care who does the comforting as long as someone does! A new infant hasn't yet developed awareness of the special people in his or her life. However, one parent's comfort may seem to be more effective.

If your infant settles down rapidly when held by the biological mother, this doesn't mean rejection of poor, ole dad! It just means the baby finds comfort in listening to the same heartbeat already heard for nine months! Also, moms often have a soft, cushiony feel as they cradle a child.

An adopted baby may find dad's heartbeat more familiar, and, therefore, more comforting. A biological child may sense the calm welcome of the father's embrace. But, both will feel the tension of an uptight, fretful, fearful, or frantic

First Days of Parenting

mom or dad who has trouble relaxing and feels awkward holding a newborn or small child.

Whether you're the father or the mother, you will have a calming, quietening effect on your child as you become calm and quiet yourself. Your baby will feel peaceful in your arms as you feel at peace with yourself, your family, and God.

Prayer: Oh, Lord, I know I worry! Sometimes I'm afraid I'll never be very good at parenting. But the more I try, the less I succeed! Help me to relax in Your embrace in Jesus' name.

Journey with God: Ask God to bring to your mind anything that keeps you from relaxing in Him. Be as specific as you can in listing your areas of concern. Pray about each one.

_____

_____

_____

_____

_____

_____

_____

_____

Day 32

*They that were foolish
took their lamps,
and took no oil with them:
But the wise took oil
in their vessels with their lamps.*

Matthew 25:3–4, KJV

One of the biggest shocks of parenthood comes as you realize, "This doesn't stop!" Unlike a nine-to-five job, parenting clocks in twenty-four hours—day after day, night after night, week after week! With no one to help, no break in routine, and no restful sleep, you'll eventually feel like running down the street, screaming, in your pajamas!

Before there's any threat of losing your sanity or your slippers, take a vacation! Okay, it's not the time for two weeks in the Bahamas, but you can vacate your premises! Just arrange a short daily outing to evacuate you from the ongoing scenery of four walls.

Even if you can only get out for a few minutes, the time helps your body, mind, and spirit function more efficiently—like the ten-minute breaks allotted other workers twice a day. Besides a change of pace and scenery, the fresh air and exercise will be healthful for you and your infant too.

Do not, however, make the mistake of grabbing up your baby and rushing out the door without any preparation. You may think, "We'll only be gone a minute or two. I don't need to bother with a diaper bag." But no one knows what surprises a day will bring! The sun may beam warmly. The squirrels may put on a show. The neighbor may invite you for a cup of tea. So, be prepared to enjoy special moments as they come. Keep a diaper bag filled with extra bottle, water, wipes, diapers, and change of clothes. Then look out! The Lord may have a lovely outing planned and ready for you!

Prayer: Dear Father, parenthood brought some moments I hadn't expected—some that aren't particularly fun! Help me to see the joys You bring to me each day in Jesus' name. Thanks!

Journey with God: Is there something fun that you miss doing? Tell God how you feel. Listen to His word to you about mini-vacations you can enjoy in your daily routine.

_____

_____

_____

_____

_____

_____

_____

_____

_____

> *For we walk by faith,
> not by sight.*
>
> 2 Corinthians 5:7, KJV

Day 33

So, what do you feel like doing—taking a nap? Surely your baby will fall asleep sometime during the day! Do you prefer taking a drive in the country or a trip to the mall, library, or museum? With an infant carrier and a well-filled diaper bag, your little one will benefit from the refreshing sights and sounds too. Would you rather take a walk in your own neighborhood? A buggy or a stroller that reclines will keep your infant (and your arms!) comfortable. Then— briskly or leisurely—you can walk at your own pace.

In these first days of parenting, your baby hasn't yet developed a pace or many preferences. As long as he or she feels fed, safe, rested, and comfortable, your child's likes or dislikes needn't concern you too much right now. However, you do need to be concerned about what you would like to do!

Even if you're the most wondrous, loving, kind parent on earth, you still have basic needs. You still require time to sleep, eat, drink, and bathe! You still need a roof over your head. You still need love and joy and peace in your life.

Some things you love to do may be on hold a while. You aren't as free to come and go as you once were, but neither are you trapped—even if it seems that way at times! Unlike your baby, you are free to decide! You have choices not yet available to a child. But, like a tiny infant, you may find your best option comes from putting your needs into the care of your Heavenly Father. So, choose to take a walk in faith! Let God guide and provide what you need to keep you strolling along, joyfully, as you ride in His will for you.

Prayer: Dear Father, help me to trust You the way my baby trusts me so completely for care. Thank You for tending to my needs in Jesus' name.

Journey with God: Do you feel stopped from doing anything because of the difficulties you see? Ask God to walk you into knowing His will for you at this particular time.

_____

_____

_____

_____

_____

_____

_____

_____

_____

_____

*Yea, though I walk through the valley
of the shadow of death,
I will fear no evil:
for thou art with me;
thy rod and thy staff
they comfort me.*

Psalm 23:4, KJV

Has the only walk you've taken lately been with a colicky infant across the nursery floor? When a baby chronically cries, squirms, and draws up with a stomachache, colic may be the problem. If so, the pediatrician can offer solutions and check out other concerns you may have.

Older babies occasionally experience discomfort or an elevated temperature before cutting teeth or after trying new foods. But infants can run a fever for no detectable reason! Sometimes, further investigation by a doctor will uncover an earache, allergy, or cold. At other times, no one really knows what's the matter.

In dark times of uncertainty, you can't help but feel alarmed. Yet, even if your child becomes quite ill, certain steps will take you from fearful reactions or inaction to an active walk in faith. For instance, if a fever rages, you can actively pray, of course, and also take action by doing what God has given you an ability to do. This might mean sponging icy water on pulse-points behind the wrists, neck, or knees to help lower the baby's temperature. Or it may mean taking your child to a doctor for medication, such as a suppository, to be inserted rectally, or drops, to be given orally.

First Days of Parenting

You may not yet have enough experience to trust your parenting instincts, but you do have experience trusting God! So, trust Him now to comfort and guide you into knowing what is best. The night may be dark, and concern for your child may drop your faith to an all-time low, but your loving Father stays with you in that valley. Fear only Him.

Prayer: Praise You, Heavenly Father, for Your almighty, all-knowing care for my family in Christ's name!

Journey with God: List your concerns about your child, and let God tell you what He knows.

_____

_____

_____

_____

_____

_____

_____

_____

_____

_____

*Thou anointest
my head
with oil.*
Psalm 23:5, KJV

Do you know the Twenty-third Psalm by heart? Have you taken it to heart as an example of parenting? The familiar picture of the Lord as Shepherd shows that His presence, His protection, and His provision permit you to take care of your family by taking God's care for you and giving it to others in your household!

God doesn't just tell you how to be a heavenly mom or dad. He shepherds you into knowing. He doesn't just expect you to give and give until you're all "give out." He provides all you need for tending your beloved lambs.

Besides the still-true picture of shepherding, the Twenty-third Psalm shows a view of God as the gracious Host for those who flock to Him. The last two verses especially demonstrate the holy Host as one who constantly stands by, giving without measure and offering a permanent residence.

Meanwhile, God has chosen you to be His host or hostess for your family—with the understanding that it's *His* family too! In Jesus' name, He's given you His authority to protect, provide for, and prepare your child for eternal life with Him.

First Days of Parenting

For now, that means little things, such as rubbing pure, unscented mineral oil, olive oil, or even vegetable oil into your baby's scalp to soothe cradle cap or dry skin! It means crooning hymns now and establishing godly standards later. It means dark days of standing fearless in discipline and firm in prayer. It means climbing out of valleys and ascending ever higher in faith as you seek your Shepherd and see that—wherever you are—God is there.

Prayer: Dear Lord, my Shepherd, I have no need but You! Help me to provide a safe and comforting environment for the child You've entrusted to me. Help me to overflow with compassion, acceptance, and love. Help my family to dwell in the place of Your goodness and mercy forever in Christ's name.

Journey with God: Even if you can quote Psalm 23 backwards, read it, prayerfully noticing every word. Then, use the above example to adapt each line into a personal prayer line for your family.

_____

_____

_____

_____

_____

_____

Every morning I tell you what I need, and I wait for your answer.

Psalm 5:3, NCV

"Good morning, Lord!"

Do you have a habit of starting your day with prayer? As with any good idea, it's easy to forget! So, right now while you're thinking about it, ask God to remind you to begin each morning, fresh, with Him.

Some days, an alarm will rudely shake you from slumber. Other times, your child's wail will startle you awake. But, just as your baby cries without any formal training or prior experience, so do you—God's child—instinctively cry for His help.

In times of emergency, weariness, and stress, the most basic prayer erupts like a wail: "God, help!" If that comes to your mind or lips, let it out! God already knows when you feel like screaming or wailing, so why not cry out to Him?

As your baby's nighttime sleep (and yours!) increases, you'll wake up gradually and refreshed. By then, you may only have a few seconds before you have to get up, but surely you can lay still long enough to offer the day to God!

For an optimum, peaceful night of rest, you've probably discovered the importance of dealing with fears or worries before you go to sleep. Therefore, each morning begins a new cycle of work, play, rest, and other activities throughout the day. Some days will go better than others, yet each stays the same: Every day, you need God. From the moment you wake, you need His answers about the decisions you make and actions you take! So for goodness' sake (and the sake of your family) begin and end each day in prayer!

Prayer: In Jesus' name, help me to remember to talk with You, Lord, before my morning even begins.

Journey with God: In the space below, remind yourself of the personal and family needs you want to discuss with God daily.

_____

_____

_____

_____

_____

_____

_____

_____

_____

_____

> *I will praise you, LORD,*
> *with all my heart.*
> *I will tell all the miracles*
> *you have done.*
> *I will be happy because of you.*
> *God Most High, I will sing praises*
> *to your name.*
>
> Psalm 9:1–2, NCV

Have you ever wondered how to praise God with all your heart? Do you think you just don't have it in you? You may be right! But that's not necessarily a chronic condition. It's a choice—yours!

For most people, praising God doesn't come easily. For new parents, it's especially hard when you're tired, worried, or not feeling particularly great. That's understandable. You have a lot of adjustments to make as you face some of the thankless tasks that come with parenting!

For example, you've already encountered various expenses through obstetric or adoption fees and your baby's pediatric care. You've had to rearrange space and furnishings in your home. You've had to shift your workload, adjust your pace, and fit your routines around your child. You're no longer free to come and go as you please; but, even if you were, you don't have the energy to go anywhere anyway!

Besides sharing these familiar experiences with most new parents, you have a unique set of circumstances to which you must adjust. You will! But don't wait until you adapt to all the changes to start each day in praise of God. Today's psalm repeatedly shows you how to begin right away! Even when your heart feels far from praise, you simply decide, "I will."

Prayer: Okay, Lord, I'm willing to say, "I will," but it's hard to believe I'll be happy and have a heart full of praise just by saying so! Is that all You need—my *willingness* to praise You? Then, praise God! I'm making that choice right now in the name of Jesus in whom I do believe!

Journey with God: To understand what praise means, think of words such as *applause, approval, admiration, adoration, commendation, celebration, glorification,* and *a standing* (or kneeling) *ovation.* Ask God to bring to mind aspects of His character that you most admire or applaud. List those as a reminder not to let His parenting of you be a thankless task!

_____

_____

_____

_____

_____

_____

_____

_____

_____

Day 38

Those who know the LORD trust him, because he will not leave those who come to him.

Psalm 9:10, NCV

The more you know God, the more you trust Him. The more you trust Him, the more you know when, how, or what to praise! In these first days of parenting, you're getting to know your baby and your ability to be a good parent. If you had (as most people do) any regrettable childhood experiences, you might have added doubts about yourself as you wonder, "Will I be just like the adults who let me down?"

So? Will you? Frankly, it isn't up to them! It's up to you! But the more you know God, the more you know He will not leave you—unless you deliberately or completely turn your back on Him.

Maybe one of your parents did completely abandon you in childhood. (God didn't.) Maybe an adult deliberately treated you badly. (God did not.) Maybe your mother or father died young. (God is very much alive, forever!)

When you think about it, you can see God has always been there for you. He's never left you. He'll be around as long as you're around—the Parent you cannot outlive or outgrow!

Like most fathers or mothers, though, God might allow circumstances that make absolutely no sense to His children! But He's not accountable to you for His decisions or actions. You're accountable to Him. He's your Heavenly Father, and you're His child. So, if He's the kind of parent you want to be, just make up your mind to take after Him.

Prayer: Thank You, Father, for never leaving me. Thank You for being the one Holy Parent I can always trust for my well-being. Help me to forgive those who haven't proven worthy of such trust. Help me to get to know You as You were, are, and will be forever in my life. Help me to trust You completely with my family and my parenting skills in Jesus' name.

Journey with God: Is it hard for you to trust God's parenting skills or your own? Ask Him to help you recall significant times in childhood when you felt abandoned, misunderstood, or mistreated by adults in some way. Ask Him to help you see Him in each memory He recovers for you now.

_____

_____

_____

_____

_____

_____

_____

Day 39

*I can lie down and go to sleep,
and I will wake up again,
because the LORD gives me strength.*

Psalm 3:5, NCV

Have you ever tried to go to sleep when you're worried about something? You probably tossed around, stared at the ceiling, or woke up, off and on, still fretting. What's really annoying, though, is waking up in the middle of the night when the baby is sleeping like a baby!

If you're inclined to worry when you need to rest, you already know the negative aspects of that trait. You know how fretting doesn't show your trust in God. You also know how easily worry leads you into fear instead of faith or rest. So you may be surprised to discover there's a good and blessed side too: *Worriers* can be great prayer *warriors!*

With the coming of a child, you have more concerns than ever. But, instead of fretting about health, money, work, rest, or relationships, take each thought, one at a time, to the Lord. Otherwise, the tendency will be to group thoughts together so they meet overhead in the middle of the night!

Usually, worry starts with caring. Because you care, you notice whatever needs fixing, mending, or healing, and that's good! That's love. But, here's where trouble comes: You start thinking, "What can I do to help?" Or "What can I do to make this better?" Then, thoughts take a twist, turning toward your abilities and inabilities, instead of heading straight for help from the one true source of good help—God!

Prayer: Heavenly Father, forgive me for turning away from You and toward myself as the solver of problems. Please help me, Lord, to give You my concerns, one at a time, throughout the day or night. Quieten my spirit for a good night's rest, and in the morning, help me to awaken, knowing what You want me to do in the name and power of Your Son, Jesus Christ.

Journey with God: Worrying often denotes a fine mind, given to observing, analyzing, or diagnosing concerns. In this space (1) List problems you've detected. (2) Ask God to give you His specific prayers for each. (3) Keep praying as He leads.

_____

_____

_____

_____

_____

_____

_____

_____

Day 40

*When you are angry,
do not sin.
Think about these
things quietly as you go to bed.*

Psalm 4:4, NCV

So how's your sex life? If you'd rather not discuss it, you might want to think about it—quietly, of course!

If you're the one who's apt to consider, analyze, and diagnose problems, you may be doing that, out of habit, as you go to bed. Since that doesn't exactly put a person in a romantic mood, your spouse may be miffed! He or she may be feeling angry or hurt that you're so busy giving attention to everything else—especially with a new baby in the house—you've forgotten the person right there beside you!

Maybe you're the one who's upset because your husband doesn't seem to understand that your body needs to recuperate a little longer after the strains of childbirth. Or, perhaps, your wife has physically recovered, but the baby keeps waking up at the most untimely moments! Or, maybe you both feel too exhausted to think about sex, and that really makes you mad!

Regardless, try to talk things out before you go to bed. Briefly state the facts as you see them, but avoid placing blame. Just say how you feel, and let your spouse respond. Listen carefully to what's said. Then pray!

Praying together brings your concerns to God and invites Him into your personal situation. In return, you receive His help, His power, His view. For example, you might suddenly understand what your partner has been trying to say. Or you may see how something you said came out all wrong.

Prayer neutralizes acid tongues and feelings! For one thing, it's hard to stay mad at someone when you're praying! Also, praying together keeps you from letting anger turn into sins of resentment, condemnation, or pride. Yet, praying provides your relationship with something more intimate than sex! It binds you together—spiritually one—with God.

Prayer: Lord, I feel a little embarrassed to pray with my spouse. Help us to come together in Jesus' name.

Journey with God: Discuss with God—and your spouse—any sore spots in your relationship.

_____

_____

_____

_____

_____

_____

_____

_____

_____

> *Thus says the LORD,
> the Holy One of Israel,
> and its Maker:
> Will you question me
> about my children,
> or command me
> concerning the work
> of my hands?*
>
> Isaiah 45:11, NRSV

"Why, God? Why?"

If your child fusses, night after night, making you too tired to give each other attention, you may be wondering *why*. The baby's fussiness could stem from an allergy, but, to be sure, discuss symptoms with a pediatrician. Also, consider the physical makeup, inherited traits, and living environment around your child.

Ask yourself, for instance, if allergies run on either side of the family. If so, you've probably had experience in avoiding certain allergens and treating symptoms that result from exposure or contact. You know what precautions to take for your child should similar conditions arise. But, you'll be glad to know that some allergies you expected might not occur at all!

Studies show that children who aren't exposed to known allergens in their first three years of life may be able to handle them later. Just because a family member is allergic to chocolate, for example, your child might not be—*if* he or she never tastes the stuff until, at least, the age of three!

Many families, however, aren't aware that frequent colds or flu-like symptoms come from allergies. They don't realize that dust, mold, mildew, pollen, pet dander, perfume, sprays, and certain foods can play havoc with sinuses. So, if runny noses, itchy eyes, wheezy coughs, or aching ears and throats frequent your house, you need to get rid of irritants. Just don't irritate God by demanding explanations or asking why! Rather, ask, "Lord, what do You want me to do?" Then do it!

Prayer: Forgive me, Lord, for questioning You about my baby's health, sensitivities, or physical makeup. Thank You for this person You created in Jesus' name.

Journey with God: Ask God to reveal any allergens, irritants, or irritating situations in your house! Discuss these with Him and other adults-in-residence.

*Woe to anyone who says to a father,
"What are you begetting?"
or to a woman,
"With what are you in labor?"*

Isaiah 45:10, NRSV

Are you making a terrible mistake? Are you blaming God, your spouse, yourself, or your parents for a condition that's troubling your baby? If so, whoa!

Instead of allowing bad feelings to reside in your home, talk with the pediatrician about specific concerns. Find out what other family members want to know too, and take along this list during your baby's one-month or six-weeks checkup.

Your questions may seem silly to you, or you may feel stupid asking, but ask anyway! The doctor won't know what's bothering you unless you give some indication. Besides, your questions might provide the needed answers about your baby's health, care, or general well-being.

Medical science and technology have undergone changes since you were a child, so, even if you've been told there's no answer for a particular problem, there may be now! Find out. Also, ask about anything that arises during the visit. For instance, if the pediatrician says to do something twice a day, does that mean exactly twelve hours apart or is there room for variation? Clarify, being as specific as you can about what you need to know.

First Days of Parenting

The doctor won't have all the answers, of course, but that's okay. You probably won't remember everything you meant to ask anyway! If you really need to know, you can always call a pediatric nurse. If it can wait, just start a new list to take for your baby's next checkup. But don't question God about His wisdom in creating your family as He did!

Prayer: Heavenly Father, I'm not always sure why You chose to make us a certain way, but most of the time I'm glad. Forgive me when I'm not. Help me not to question Your goodness but to accept each person in my family as we are in Jesus' name.

Journey with God: List family woes, discussing them with God.

Day 43

*God, examine me
and know my heart;
test me and know
my nervous thoughts.
See if there is any bad thing in me.
Lead me on the road
to everlasting life.*

Psalm 139:23–24, NCV

Do you feel nervous about taking your baby to the doctor for a checkup? As the pediatrician examines your child, you may feel as if your parenting skills are under observation too! Naturally, you want to know what's needed for your baby's well-being, but you may also want to know, "Hey, Doc, am I doing okay? Do I pass the test?"

You're probably doing just fine! That's likely because you've continued to bless your family with your sincerity in following God and seeking Him each day in this devotional time. But things can still come up that you have difficulty handling! Right now, for instance, that could be seeing your baby get his or her first shot. Most parents flinch at the sight. Some turn away, unable to watch. Others burst into tears. But, with God's help, your nervousness won't upset or alarm your child. As soon as you see that needle coming, pray!

Ask the Lord to help you help your baby. Ask Him to calm you so you can calm your child. Don't fake a smile or pretend everything is great when it isn't! Just rub the spot as you talk softly to your little one. Then do what you can to end the visit on a pleasant note—to reassure your baby now and set the tone for future trips to the doctor's office.

In case you're still wondering how you're doing, be assured of this: Each time you pray to the Lord and listen to His response, you pass His test of your parenting skill! As God examines your thoughts and heart, what He's looking for is something of Himself in you.

Prayer: Dear Lord, please help my baby—and me—get past this first checkup just fine. Keep us filled with Your Holy Spirit in Jesus' name.

Journey with God: Is anything hindering God's Spirit in you or your family's life? Discuss this with God.

Day 44

Let this be recorded for a generation to come, so that a people yet unborn may praise the LORD.

Psalm 102:18, NRSV

"My, how big you've grown!" Unless a medical concern hinders rapid growth, your baby has lengthened and gained weight these last few weeks. How much weight and how many inches depend on inherited characteristics which may already be apparent. A long, thin baby, for example, may stay thin simply because both parents are inclined to be lean 'n lanky!

Expect growth spurts to alternate with level periods as your child adjusts to other physical changes too. When babies begin to teethe, for instance, they're less likely to put on inches or ounces. Level periods also occur as a child starts to sit up, crawl, or walk. It's as though the body says, "One thing at a time, please!"

As you see changes in your child, note them in the baby book. Your regular visits to the pediatrician's office can help remind you to log in height, weight, date, shots, and other information too. Date photographs you want to include, and, later, record the cute things your child says or does.

"Tell me about when I was little," your child will say someday, and you'll bring out the baby book as a reminder of all you want to share. Especially during preschool days, your son or daughter will love for you to "read" this favorite picture book—a picture of his or her life. Yet, this won't be complete without at least a glimpse of God's work too! So, as you update the baby book, be sure to record acts of faith and answered prayers. Let this be a reminder of God's child care in your family for generations yet to come.

Prayer: God, bless my family—now and future generations too—with a clear picture of Your love in Jesus' name.

Journey with God: Ask God to help you recall and record some of the many times He's blessed your family.

> *And God said,
> "Behold, I have given you
> every herb bearing seed,
> which is upon the face
> of all the earth, and every tree,
> in which is the fruit
> of a tree yielding seed.*
>
> Genesis 1:29, KJV

So, when's the last time you had a physical? If you're the biological mom, you've probably scheduled a one-month or six-weeks follow-up visit with your obstetrician. This gives you an opportunity to find out how you're progressing and to ask questions before you resume your normal activities. You might also ask about diet and vitamin supplements, especially if you're breast-feeding. If you're still feeling blue, you might discuss that with your doctor too.

As the father or adopting parent, though, don't think you get out of a check-up! Your family needs you. You owe them—and yourself—attention to your health. This may mean facing concerns by asking questions and getting answers. If a doctor doesn't explain information to your satisfaction, find someone who does! Or research your questions with books and articles written by several reputable sources.

Many people walk around, not ill, but not really well. Often, low energy comes from poor nutrition. Take-out food has too many nutrients taken out or too much grease put in! A body needs water, fiber, vitamins, and minerals from well-balanced meals with lots of fresh fruit and vegetables, grains (corn, oat, rice, wheat), herbs (parsley, basil, sage, mustard seed, fennel, garlic), or natural food supplements.

God created everything needed for naturally good health! He provided plants for medicinal use. He provided doctors to diagnose and prescribe. He provided preventative medicine in the fresh produce section of your grocery store!

Prayer: Creator God, thank You for providing care and healing for my body, mind, and spirit. Help me to find the answers I need for my family's nourishment in Jesus' name.

Journey with God: Have you noticed how God color-coordinated food? If you've been eating monotone meals, you may need to add more dark green, yellow, and red vegetables or fruit! Write down thoughts God gives you on color-balancing meals.

_____

_____

_____

_____

_____

_____

_____

_____

Day 46

The wife hath not power of her own body, but the husband: and likewise also the husband hath not power of his own body, but the wife.

1 Corinthians 7:4, KJV

With a new baby in the house, do you ever feel as though your body isn't your own? Well, guess what? It wasn't yours anyway! If you're married, your body belongs to your spouse!

Owning each other doesn't mean that God endorsed slavery when He signed your wedding vows! It means you value your marriage partner's well-being at least as much as your own. That's true for your spouse too: You become more important to him or her than you are to yourself.

For example, if your partner says, "Honey, I wish you'd get more rest," or, "Please eat more nutritiously," you'd better listen! Ignoring the warning or making excuses won't improve your health—or your marriage! Neither will spouting off and saying something like, "Hey! Who gave you the right to tell me what to do?" Well, God did, that's who!

Your Heavenly Father did not mean, of course, for these physical rights to be misused or abused. He never sanctioned name-calling, slapping someone around, or forcing sex on an unconsenting partner. His love doesn't hurt anyone! It tends and mends.

God did, however, give you every right to let your spouse know when you're interested in physical love-making. And, since you're more concerned about your partner's body than your own, God knows you'll take your spouse's wants and needs into consideration too. Wow! Look what God started with this—equality in marriage!

Prayer: Dear loving Father, thank You for coming up with such a brilliant plan! Please help it to work well in my marriage and family in Jesus' name.

Journey with God: Has your partner fussed at you lately about the way you take care of yourself? Have you complained or worried about him or her? Discuss your family's physical well-being with God and your spouse.

Day 47

*So then, rid yourselves of all evil,
all lying, hypocrisy, jealousy,
and evil speech.
As newborn babies want milk,
you should want the pure
and simple teaching.
By it you can grow up
and be saved.*

1 Peter 2:1, NCV

Did you hope that having a baby would draw you and your spouse closer together? Have you found that, after weeks of sleep loss and tiredness, the opposite has occurred? Have you said things to each other that you regretted? Or, have you always been so close that one of you now feels jealous of the attention the other gives the baby?

Babies have been known to make both parents grow up, fast! For one thing, it's no longer as easy to be concerned only about yourself! A crying infant won't let you! But, neither will your love. You do love one another, right? That doesn't necessarily mean intensely hot *passion* but intense *compassion!* Love means caring about another person as much as you do about yourself—and behaving accordingly.

Now is such a blessed time, it can draw you closer together. But it's also a weary, uncertain "What do we do?" time. So, instead of focusing on yourself and the letdown you feel after weeks of expectancy, give yourselves a break! Let each other recover a personal loss of strength, and your passion will soon strengthen too!

First Days of Parenting

Especially, boost your energy (and your relationship) by ridding yourselves of any tiresome jealousies or resentments. Don't lie or deny your feelings—that would be hypocritical! But speak honestly about anything that bothers you, giving each problem to the Lord. Let Him help you grow up in Him!

Prayer: Dear Father, sometimes we both act so childishly! Thank You for helping our relationship become full grown in Your love for us in Jesus' name.

Journey with God: Ask God to bring to your mind anything that keeps you from wanting to grow up. Pray about whatever seems to thwart your mental and spiritual process.

So if anyone is in Christ, there is a new creation: everything old has passed away; see, everything has become new!

2 Corinthians 5:17, NRSV

"But that's what we've always done!"

With the coming of a new creation to your family, you've seen old schedules and viewpoints pass away. Just because you used to do something a certain way doesn't mean you still can—or even want to!

Babies often change their parents' view of many things. Days and nights get all mixed up. Theories turn into reality. Wants give way to needs, and what's practical takes priority over what's planned. Yet, into the middle of this upheaval, come previously untapped strength, honesty, and spontaneity.

"The baby's taking a nap. Do you want to do the same?"

"If you need to rest, sure. Otherwise, I'd rather enjoy the quiet and just be with you."

No longer taken for granted, peaceful times alone become more precious. They provide an opportunity to recollect lost energy and give brief moments to express what you think and feel—something your marriage partner cannot possibly know unless you say! This could mean discussing something you've recently thought about or realized. But, with precious few minutes, there's no time for lengthy discussions or debates!

First Days of Parenting

In the moments you have alone together, get to what's important! Let mind reading, self-centeredness, and old expectations pass away! Embrace each other. Show affection. Give loving attention. And, make sure your spouse knows how much he or she means to you—not just as a marriage partner, but as the new mother or father of your child.

Prayer: Dear Lord, help our relationship to be renewed and made whole in Jesus' name.

Journey with God: Talk with God about any aspect of your marriage that's troubling you. Ask Him to give you His words in approaching a specific subject with your spouse.

Day 49

To every thing there is a season, and a time to every purpose under the heaven.

Ecclesiastes 3:1, KJV

Have you or your spouse been thinking about going back to work? Many new mothers do for many valuable reasons, such as income, personal satisfaction, a challenging career, the contribution made to society, or a calling on one's life.

No matter what the reasons are or what decision is made, you'll discover a sacrifice involved. For instance, if both of you work in a salaried position, you'll have more income, but less time with your baby and less say-so in small matters throughout the day. If one of you stays home, that person may lose interesting work or career advancement. If you alternate working hours so your child is home around the clock, you'll have less time for each other's company.

Some parents find alternatives, such as a career that allows you to work from your home. But your baby's needs and other interruptions will, at times, hinder your concentration or your ability to do your job. So this also means sacrifice as you try to make yourself available each second of the day!

Are you beginning to see there's no ideal solution which suits everyone? Do you see that only you, your spouse, and

First Days of Parenting

God can know what's right in your situation? Can you also see the hope of a time, a season, for all that you want or need to do?

God knows the desires of your heart. He knows how much you care about your family. He knows the work He's given you. He knows what can wait and what cannot! So, talk with Him about your unique set of circumstances. Discuss it with your spouse, and pray. Together—with the Lord—you'll know what it really is time to do, whatever that may be.

Prayer: Heavenly Father, thank You for Your provisions for us. Thank You for letting us know what we're to do and when. Please guide us into what's best for our family and pleasing to You in Jesus' name.

Journey with God: List the pros and cons about the choices you face in your particular situation. Pray about each one.

___

___

___

___

___

___

___

___

> *What gain have the workers from their toil?*
>
> Ecclesiastes 3:9, NRSV

Have you checked out the daycare centers in your area? If your church sponsors such a program, you probably know what you'll do about reliable care for your baby. If not, you might ask church members, friends, and relatives what they've experienced or heard about local facilities.

Some daycare centers don't allow infants, preferring to tend only pre-schoolers who have been potty-trained. But those who do accept babies should have adequate space between cribs and an ample ratio of workers to handle each child's needs. You should also see rocking chairs, diaper-changing areas, and evidence of cleanliness everywhere you look!

As you check out facilities, ask about each center's methods of operation, schedules, and compliance with safety requirements and government regulations. If they've received commendations, you can certainly expect to hear about that! But also ask if they've ever been cited for anything.

If possible, chat briefly with each caretaker. Frequent turnovers can indicate that something isn't quite right, so find out how long each person has worked there. Ask new workers about their previous employment too, keeping the conversation cordial and light.

You might not uncover anything a center wishes to hide, but you will sense the atmosphere and prevalent attitudes as you walk around the place. Do workers seem happy being with young children? Do they seem to receive something valuable from their work? Do you feel at ease there? Do you know God cares about your child's welfare? Trust Him to guide.

Prayer: Heavenly Father, I'm having doubts about letting anyone take care of my baby but me! Please quieten my fears, and help me to hear You as You guide me in Jesus' name.

Journey with God: Write down what you've observed in touring a daycare facility or interviewing a potential baby-sitter. List the positives and negatives, discussing each with God.

_____

_____

_____

_____

_____

_____

_____

_____

Day 51

*They will perish, but you endure;
they will all wear out like a garment.*

Psalm 102:26, NRSV

Clothes were meant to wear out—diapers included! That may seem strange until you consider the alternatives. How do you feel, for instance, about your baby's dirty diapers still being around for his or her great-great-great-grandchildren to see? That's not a pretty picture! Yet this happens to so-called "disposable" diapers, which, as it turns out, are not usually disposable at all!

When you first brought your baby home, you probably needed the help of throw-away diapers. They decreased your workload, kept your newborn dry, and protected the umbilical cord in a well-fitted, sanitized wrapping. You might still need to have them when you're traveling. But, as your baby and energy grow, plastic diapers can become a convenience that's inconvenient for others in centuries to come!

Instead of having what's relatively out of sight now in the sight of future relatives, consider the advantages of cloth diapers: They "breathe" more, so they don't seal in bacteria that foster rashes and infections. They can be handed down to the next baby in the family, yet your child's descendants won't have to deal with them!

First Days of Parenting

Some things are meant to last. Some aren't. If that's confusing, ask God to help you discern the difference. Ask Him about the permanence of His Word and why some people seem too quick to dispose of it! Ask Him to reveal to you anything that hinders you from seeing His enduring truths and values as expressed in His Word and Son.

Prayer: Heavenly Father, the world's value system seems so different from Yours! I'm not always sure when You disagree with what I've learned or thought was okay. I guess I'd be less confused if I knew the Bible really really really well! So help me to read Your Word each day and better understand Your standards and truths in Jesus' name.

Journey with God: Do you like to read? If so, reading the Bible, cover to cover, will take about as much time as a long novel! If you're not fond of reading, make a commitment to complete a chapter or at least a small portion of Scripture daily. Ask God about His personal requirement for you.

Day 52

For last night there stood by me an angel of the God to whom I belong and whom I worship.

Acts 27:23, NRSV

If you want your baby to have cloth diapers but don't know how you'll find extra time for laundry, check into a diaper service. Compare the cost against what you'd pay for throw-aways. If you have a housekeeper, maid, baby-sitter, or nursery assistant, ask what additional charge there'd be for diaper-washing, drying, and folding.

You may think it's as hard to find good help as it is to discover an angel in disguise, but neither are difficult for God to produce! He knows what you need and when. So He'll provide what's best for your family's care and well-being.

When circumstances necessitate it, God has been known to bring forth angelic help, but this doesn't come from recycled humans who have died! Supernaturally, angels are spiritual beings, created as such by God. They'll never be human, and you'll never be an angel! But, you worship one Creator—God.

Angels have unique work, such as giving people messages from the Lord, fighting spiritual battles, or doing a host of other jobs in a spiritual realm. Therefore, angels don't hire themselves out for wages, but nice people do!

Although you won't find angels through a classified ad, you might locate heavenly household help! So, pray about it. Make a budget that considers your family's needs. Ask your friends to recommend laundry help or a diaper service. Then, let God stand by you, naturally and supernaturally too!

Prayer: Dear Heavenly Father, thank You for helping me to find the help I need to take care of my family. If that means giving me the time or energy to do more physical work myself, that's fine too! Just let me know Your priorities. Help me not to hold in high esteem little conveniences that don't matter at all to You. Help me to worship only You in Jesus' name.

Journey with God: Did your new baby bring extra work? What household chores seem especially burdensome? Discuss these with God, and listen for His solutions.

_____

_____

_____

_____

_____

_____

_____

Day 53

*Only be careful,
and watch yourselves closely
so that you do not forget the things
your eyes have seen
or let them slip from your heart
as long as you live.*

Deuteronomy 4:9, NIV

Is your baby starting to turn over? For most newborns, large pillows can keep your infant from rolling off a bed or sofa and onto the floor. Just be careful, of course, that breathing won't be obstructed by any objects you place around your child.

As your baby becomes more mobile, you may want to invest in a playpen. Or, perhaps you could arrange a safe, clean, carpeted area with bumper pads set around to keep your child enclosed. The idea isn't to confine but to protect your baby from rolling into the furniture, fireplace, lamps, and other rough, sharp, hard, or potentially dangerous objects.

Even in a well-constructed, cozy playpen, however, your infant will still need watching. He or she will want to watch you too! By being close enough to see what you're doing throughout the day, your baby will be included, entertained, and also quick to learn!

As you go from room to room, look for a safe, out-of-the way place to set your child in a secured seat or on a clean, uncluttered spot on the floor. If the playpen can easily be transported from one room to another, set it anywhere you plan to be for more than a few minutes. Then, you two can keep an eye on each other, just as God keeps an eye on you! You've heard, of course, that God watches you all of the time. He does! But, like you, He doesn't prefer to see what's wrong with His child! He loves and cares about you so much, He wants to protect you, enjoy your company, and not let you out of His sight!

Prayer: Dear Father, in Jesus' name, help me not to lose sight of You.

Journey with God: Have you written down things you don't want to forget about God's help, love, and care for your family? Use this space to help you recall what you've seen Him do!

_____

_____

_____

_____

_____

_____

_____

_____

_____

_____

> But take care and watch yourselves closely, so as neither to forget the things that your eyes have seen nor to let them slip from your mind all the days of your life; make them known to your children and your children's children.
>
> Deuteronomy 4:9, NRSV

Babies like bright objects. They're drawn to strong colors and shiny things, such as car keys and eyeglasses—neither of which belong in their little mouths!

Appropriate toys for your baby depend on his or her abilities and awareness. For instance, an infant who likes to clutch things or wave a little fist, might enjoy shaking a brightly colored rattle—one that also makes an interesting noise. An older baby might like to check out that cute little face in a shiny aluminum mirror—one with the edges safely rounded or enclosed in a brightly colored plastic frame.

Most parents who buy toys for their children take care to find sturdy, safe items with no easily broken or small parts that can damage little eyes, ears, noses, or mouths. Parents also want toys that don't frighten their children or represent something they themselves abhor—weapons, wizards, drolls, etc. That's as it should be when you're looking for toys, but don't stop there!

Instead of focusing on what you would never buy for your baby, concentrate on items that represent your beliefs. For example, if you're buying a stuffed animal, why not get a lamb to remind you of the Lamb? Or how about making a crib mobile with a cross, heart, fish, dove, and other Christian symbols? The toys you buy can be a reminder of all the wonderful things you want to tell your child someday!

Prayer: Dear God, help me to fill my home with reminders of Your presence in Jesus' name.

Journey with God: What sights, sounds, and smells remind you of God's work in your family or throughout history? Ask God about the ways you can incorporate these reminders into the nursery and rest of your home.

_____

_____

_____

_____

_____

_____

_____

_____

_____

_____

_____

_____

Let us look only to Jesus, the One who began our faith and who makes it perfect. He suffered death on the cross. But he accepted the shame as if it were nothing because of the joy that God put before him. And now he is sitting at the right side of God's throne.

Hebrews 12:2, NCV

Throughout the centuries, artists have rendered drawings of Jesus as they supposed Him to look, but the ones that seem the most true-to-life are those that show Him in action. For example, Jesus talking with the children, walking on water, feeding a multitude of people, or stretching out His hand to heal are powerful pictures that help to remind your family of His work in your lives too.

As you look for faith-building reminders of God's power and presence in your home and nursery, find aids that help you keep your eyes on Jesus. A picture or cross has no power, but they bring to mind the One who does!

Since you don't want to shut the Lord out of any room, consider placing appropriate reminders throughout your house. Illustrations of Christ's love, for example, fit especially well into your child's nursery. Most preschoolers will be too young, of course, to understand the supreme, loving sacrifice Christ made on the cross; but even infants can respond to Jesus' smile as He welcomes little children.

By setting a picture into a protective sleeve, such as those used for photographs, you can place an illustration of Jesus' love near the crib. Or, let your baby hold a smaller picture while you change a diaper. Then, instead of wrinkling a nose at odors, you'll be inclined to say, "Jesus loves ___" (your child's name). Such practices help you aim little eyes toward Jesus from the very first days of your baby's life.

Prayer: Heavenly Father, help me to keep my eyes on You and not on the problems around me. Thank You for Your ongoing work in my family's life in Jesus' name.

Journey with God: Look around your home. What do you see? Is there evidence of a Christian family living here? Ask God to give you His impression of each room. Do you feel He wants you to include reminders that point to Him? If so, what?

_____

_____

_____

_____

_____

_____

_____

_____

_____

_____

_____

Lo, children are an heritage of the LORD: and the fruit of the womb is his reward.

Psalm 127:3, KJV

Have you been thinking about your own childhood and the kind of home your parents provided? If Christian symbols, family devotionals, Bible reading, daily prayers, and church attendance marked your early years, you have quite a heritage to pass on to your child!

In giving you a family, God passes on a heritage of blessing to you. He provides for you; you provide for your baby; and, Lord willing, your child will someday provide for others. But, as with any inheritance, you cannot give to your family (or anyone else) what you don't already own yourself!

To give, you first have to receive. So, ask yourself if you've embraced the gifts God has given you. Have you, for example, taken hold of the good news that God forgives and accepts you—not because of your own worth, but because of the worthy gift of His Son, Jesus Christ?

By yourself, you have a pretty paltry inheritance to pass on to your child—a heritage of sin! Except for Jesus, it's that way for everyone. People cannot save themselves from flaws and imperfections. They cannot make things right, but Jesus can. Only He can restore your relationship, your kinship, and your childhood with your Heavenly Father.

First Days of Parenting

As you think about the things you want to pass on to your child someday, consider God's ongoing provision. Through the life, death, and resurrection of the Lord Jesus Christ, He provides an inheritance of eternal life for you! He's made this same provision for your whole family too. Pass it on.

Prayer: Heavenly Father, my family's physical and mental needs take so much of my attention, sometimes I forget our spiritual needs. Thank You for providing fully for each of us as You tend our bodies, minds, and spirits. Help me to pass on to my family the blessings of Your love at work in me in Jesus' name.

Journey with God: Regardless of your family background, what heritage do you choose for your child? List these valuables to ensure a reminder of the gifts you want to give.

_____

_____

_____

_____

_____

_____

_____

_____

Day 57

Now faith is being sure of what we hope for and certain of what we do not see.

Hebrews 11:1, NIV

Few parents want to pass on a legacy of debt! They don't want to hand down doctor bills and funeral expenses. They'd much rather spare their children unnecessary grief by tending to such matters themselves. Yet, by the time they think about it, their insurance rates may have increased so sharply, it causes them financial pain!

In these early years of parenting, you'll find the best buys on life and health insurance. You might have excellent company benefits or a group rate available through your place of employment, and, if so, you probably can't beat the price. Otherwise, you can purchase personal insurance at a much less expensive rate than it will cost when you are older.

Either way, there's a catch! Whether you pay a lot or a little for an insurance policy, it won't insure one thing if the company goes out of business or reneges on claims! To be well-insured, you need a reputable company you have faith in—one you can trust to do what it says.

That may be an old company or a new one. So make it your policy to investigate the reputation and rating of each. Or look for a trustworthy agent who represents various insurance companies and can make solid, sensible recommendations based on your family's income, needs, and goals. Since that also means placing your faith in something or someone, find out if the insurance representative represents Christ!

No one knows for sure if another person will act on his or her beliefs. No one knows how long an individual or a company will stay in business. No one knows when health care or research will improve. Yet you can *always* know to trust God! Put your faith in Him and His ability to lead you.

Prayer: Lord, I'm sure of You. I'm certain of Your ability to guide me in the direction I'm to go in Jesus' name. Thanks!

Journey with God: Do you easily or uneasily place faith in other people, business, and government? How readily do you put your faith in God? Talk with Him about making any needed adjustments in your policies of assurance and insurance!

_____

_____

_____

_____

_____

_____

_____

> *Children should not have to save up
> to give to their parents.
> Parents should save to give
> to their children.*
>
> 2 Corinthians 12:14, NCV

With a new baby in the house, you probably don't even want to think about spending more money! So how about giving thought to saving it?

The type of savings program you need will depend on your family's budget, goals, and available options. For example, if you or your spouse work for a firm that offers a stock purchase program or a realistic retirement plan, you might check into the present costs and eventual payouts you can expect. How much would you need to put into such a program to accomplish what you want?

If you're self-employed or work for someone who doesn't have the options you need, talk with a reputable financial advisor—preferably someone who represents more than one bank or business. By agreeing to set aside a modest sum each month, you'll eventually have monies from which to draw.

That's what money is for—to be used! This can mean spending it, saving it, or sharing it, depending on what's called for at the time. But, your use of money now will help your child in years to come. Or, it won't!

You can't control unexpected expenses or every emergency that will arise, but you can make a decision to pro-

First Days of Parenting

vide for your child by doing what you can to provide for yourself! You can set aside what you're able to ignore from each paycheck, even if it's just a few dollars. You can also choose not to set aside God's Word on money matters! Just look up related topics in a concordance, and discover God's financial view!

Prayer: Heavenly Father, help me to put my money where my beliefs are—in Your Word—in Jesus' name.

Journey with God: Go over your family budget with God.

Day 59

If ye then, being evil, know how to give good gifts unto your children, how much more shall your Father which is in heaven give good things to them that ask?

Matthew 7:11, KJV

Occasionally, people make unhealthy choices. Instead of seeking what's wholesome, constructive, and healing, they settle for something injurious to their mental, physical, or spiritual well-being. That's too bad! Yet, when it comes to their children, most parents consistently choose what's good.

Usually, a healthy choice for your child also helps you. For example, as you budget today's income with tomorrow's needs in mind, you'll probably consider purchasing insurance on your baby's behalf. Such a policy can begin coverage now at a relatively inexpensive rate that your child can later assume as an adult. Meanwhile, the insurance helps to protect your family's present financial concerns.

Most likely, your insurance representative will suggest some form of whole life policy. It gives the agent a larger commission and can provide a workable solution for you if you have difficulty saving money that you might need later.

For instance, you might already be concerned about your child's education but keep forgetting to save part of each paycheck in an annuity or savings account. A whole life insurance policy on you or your spouse can help—

assuming an adequate cash buildup becomes available by the time your son or daughter enrolls in college or vocational school. You want to provide well for your baby and give good gifts, and so you will! How much more, then, do you suppose your Heavenly Father wants to give His goodness to you?

Prayer: Dear Father, thank You for the good gift of Your Holy Spirit, given to me in Jesus' name. Help me to receive more and more of You into every part of my life.

Journey with God: List God's good gifts that help you live, abundantly, in Him. Notice how these gifts are the exact opposite of *evil*—which comes from living backwards and from turning around His Word: live!

_____

_____

_____

_____

_____

_____

_____

_____

> *Honor thy father and mother; which is the first commandment with promise; That it may be well with thee, and thou mayest live long on the earth.*
>
> Ephesians 6:2–3, KJV

For most parents, buying gifts, providing necessities, and saving money all just come with the job. So does saving relationships for the next generation to enjoy!

Now that you're a parent, you may feel you understand your own parents much better—or much worse! You may see how things that used to bother you suddenly make sense or now seem insignificant. But, you might also find your parents' choices, words, or actions so inexcusable, you excuse yourself from further contact with them! That's tempting—perhaps understandable—but such a choice can bring dishonor.

Disagreeing with your parents' choices or even disliking their personalities doesn't mean you dishonor those who gave you birth or brought you up. People in the closest families will, from time to time, differ, annoy one another, or get on each other's nerves! But those who honor their father and mother value fatherhood and motherhood—and the one Heavenly Parent who created both!

As a father or mother now yourself, you've had to make decisions you'd never before faced. Sometimes that's hard—and you've just begun! So, give your parents the benefit of no longer doubting them. Give them your honor, love, and forgiveness—three choices that won't negate your feelings but will direct the actions you take!

If your parents don't deserve much respect, they may not seem to care! But someday you'll be thankful you chose to set an example for your child by valuing parenthood. Lifelong, honorable, and loving relationships will set well with thee!

Prayer: God, bless my parents! Help me always to respect and value them in a manner that honors You in Jesus' name.

Journey with God: Ask God for His light on your family's relationships.

Day 61

And the child's father and mother were amazed at what was being said about him.

Luke 2:33, NRSV

Parents say the most amazing things! Sometimes, yours may mean to tell you, "You're doing a great job! I'm so glad you're a parent now. Thank you for giving me a grandchild!" But, even if that's what they think (and they probably do), they might forget to say so.

Instead, your parents or in-laws may say, "Now see what you've done! You've made the baby cry!" (as though you'd deliberately do such a thing!). Or, "What's the matter with this child?" (as though you're to blame for anything wrong!). Or, "Here, let me show you how to do that," (as though you're incorrigible, unteachable, uncaring, or unbelievably dumb!).

As a parent yourself, you can vow not to pass on similar remarks to your child, but by the time your baby reaches your age, you'll forget! You'll be more likely to hand down what's been handed to you. You'll give what you've been given.

Although you cannot change a parent (nor do you have the right to do so!) you can change your response. You can decide to accept advice, even correction, with good humor and good grace. If circumstances make that impossible, you

First Days of Parenting

can state how criticism makes you feel, taking care not to criticize the other person in the process!

Quite probably, your mother, father, or in-laws do love your family. After all, it's their family too! So, if you listen to what's really said, you may find they're not making only negative statements about your parenting skills. They're also saying lovely and loving things about their grandchild, aren't they? Take those remarks as a word of encouragement meant for you!

Prayer: So, how am I doing, Lord? Help me to hear what You have to say about my child and my parenting skills.

Journey with God: Have you noted any critical remarks about your parenting ability? Offer that list and your decision to forgive to God. Then write in your heart, on your mind, and on this page His encouraging word that comes to you through Scripture—and any good word that others have to say!

_____

_____
_____
_____
_____
_____
_____

*God is my protection.
He makes my way free from fault.*
Psalm 18:32, NCV

Okay, here's the real world of parenting: You've already made mistakes, or you eventually will! However, you can take that negative statement as a positive word!

For one thing, you need to know that everyone makes mistakes—even the kindest, most loving, thoughtful, caring parent. Your mother or father didn't raise you without flaws! Your grandparents didn't prove themselves perfect in the job, nor did their ancestors before them. That's just how it is. But that does not excuse your mistakes!

God knew you'd get too tired and be too cranky. He knew you'd forget to place your hand behind a diaper pin or fall asleep right when your baby wanted to be fed. He knew you'd say or do something you wish you could take back. He knew you would occasionally feel down on yourself, your child, your family—or Him! Yet, knowing these things about you, God still does not give up on you or say, "Well, this one's hopeless!" Your Heavenly Father isn't a fault-finder! He's a fault-freer!

Instead of beating yourself over any oversight, botch, or blunder you've made, remind yourself that God took your errors into account before they even happened! Through the perfect sacrifice of His perfect Son, Jesus, He created a redemption plan that cannot fail. But you can fail to receive it for yourself—not by messing up but by failing to confess your mistakes to Him! So, from the start of your parenting days, give up any thought of being a Super Mom or Dad! Be glad that the one holy and perfect Parent makes you faultless by His forgiveness! Then seek His Way for carefree days of no-fault parenting of your child.

Prayer: Heavenly Father, praise You for forgiving me and restoring me wholly to You in Jesus' name.

Journey with God: Do you feel like a botched parent? Confess any mistakes you know you've made. Then, ask God to show you how He would like to be your child's mom or dad through you!

_____

_____

_____

_____

_____

_____

_____

_____

_____

_____

*When I kept things to myself,
I felt weak deep inside me.
I moaned all day long.*

Psalm 32:3, NCV

Hopefully, you've had a recent physical. But have you had a recent mental or spiritual exam? Here's a quick one you can give yourself: Ask, "How have I been feeling?"

If, like the psalmist, you've felt weak or moped and moaned around, you may need to ask yourself a couple more questions: (1) "Have I done something wrong that I haven't confessed to God?" (2) "Has someone done something wrong to me, but I didn't confess that it bothered me?"

Your own unconfessed sin—or resentment over someone else's—may be making you feel weak, inside and out! So, 'fess up! Don't hold any bitterness or remorse inside. Get rid of every dreg—the sooner, the better!

This doesn't mean dredging up anything irrelevant to the present situation. Nor does it mean spewing all over anyone or getting fussy—not even with yourself and certainly not with your baby! To confess simply means acknowledging a wrongdoing by stating and admitting the facts as you recall them. If other people are involved, you can listen to their view of the situation too, giving as much consideration to their thoughts and feelings as you have to your own.

Confession means "owning up"—not just by admitting a mistake but also in owning your feelings, perspective, and the conclusions you've reached about yourself or another person. But, then comes the good part! You're free. By confessing that sin or resentment, it no longer owns you! You're rid of it—forever—in Christ's name.

Prayer: Dear Lord, I don't like making mistakes or creating problems, so I hate to admit when that happens! I guess other people feel the same. Please help me to be quick to forgive and quick to receive Your forgiveness in Christ's name.

Journey with God: Ask God to remind you of anything you're ashamed of or have tried to keep hidden from Him, yourself, or the people around you.

Day 64

> LORD, *don't correct me
> when you are angry.
> Don't punish me
> when you are furious.*
>
> Psalm 38:1, NCV

Aren't you glad that God doesn't go around beating you over the head with your mistakes? He could, you know! His holiness demands justice. Yet this just God also has mercy, love, compassion, and forgiveness for His children. Instead of treating you like an enemy or giving what's deserved, He gently convicts you of wrongdoing and lovingly corrects.

At the moment, your son or daughter doesn't know what's right or wrong, so the only choices or actions you have to correct are your own! For example, you cannot correct your child's need to cry. That's natural, normal, and nothing to reprimand or change. So, if you're frustrated by the constant cries, it's up to you to alter not your feelings, but your actions or response.

If your baby often cries from hunger, for instance, you might add barley or rice cereal to your child's diet to help a tummy that doesn't seem to fill up on milk. If your baby seems to need extra amounts of comfort, you might allow more rocking time. If you suspect your own distraught nerves upset your baby, you might just need to rest, get a baby-sitter, or listen to your favorite instrumental hymns more often.

First Days of Parenting

God doesn't get mad at you for being human! Nor does He want you to be angry with your baby for being a baby! He knows your limitations and those of your child. So, turn to Him with prayer, praise, and thanksgiving. Seek His guidance and His strength for each day. Let Him correct you gently, and you'll spare yourself the punishment which eventually comes to those who refuse to hear Him and obey.

Prayer: Heavenly Father, thank You for Your mercy and the gentle way You have of pointing out my mistakes. Help me to hear and heed You quickly in Christ's name.

Journey with God: Are you trying to correct things about your child, family, or self which cannot be changed? Or, are you accepting things about yourself and other people which could be improved with God's help? Ask Him what to alter—and what to put on His altar!

_____

_____

_____

_____

_____

_____

_____

*They have no speech or words;
they have no voice to be heard.
But their message goes out
through all the world.*

Psalm 19:3–4, NCV

Child abuse.... The phrase makes you shudder as you hear examples of physical, mental, or spiritual abuse children have endured. Deprivation, sexual encounters, harsh beatings, and satanic rites have brutalized young people, including babies who can do nothing to defend themselves. With no speech or language, their voices cannot be heard unless people hear their cries and commit to stopping this outrage.

In some ways, most people have been victimized, whether that involves abhorrent practices, such as incest, or less obvious but harmful habits, such as name-calling or putdowns. Regardless, everyone you know needs prayer!

Without the Savior, what hope is there for children of any age? Without God's Holy Spirit, what strength or power is there to correct any situation? Without God's Word, what standard is there to know what's right or wrong?

Personally, there's not much chance you'll get around to visiting everyone who's suffered some type of abuse. Chances are, you don't have monies to provide for the protection or loving, custodial care everyone needs! However, the newscasts you watch, the headlines you read, and the stories you hear all offer you the opportunity to effect change.

You can't do much about the whole world's ills all by yourself, but you can let each word of abuse be a reminder to offer specific people and situations to God in prayer. Then you've done what's most effective anyway! You've invited God into the lives of those who have a desperate need for Him.

Prayer: Dear God, forgive me for shutting my eyes or ears to anything terrible or unpleasant. Be with those who suffer, and show them Your way in Jesus' name.

Journey with God: Have you heard upsetting news about people who can't verbalize their complaints? Intercede in prayer for the infants, pre-schoolers, unborn, disabled, and elderly persons you know who are not being heard.

For I the LORD your God am a jealous God, punishing children for the iniquity of parents, to the third and the fourth generation of those who reject me, but showing steadfast love to the thousandth generation of those who love me and keep my commandments.
Exodus 20:5–6, NRSV

Were you a victim of child abuse? Do you now fear the added punishment of perpetuating the abusiveness against you by eventually doing to your baby what was done to you? You have every reason to be concerned! Indeed, you have received a sentence of passing on the sins of your father, mother, and grandparents to your child—*if you reject God* in your life.

Each generation has legitimate complaints against the one before it. Each then fears its own ability to pass on abusive practices, unhealthy choices, poor parenting skills, ineffective discipline, and unloving attitudes. However, each generation—each individual family member—has the ability to break this weighty chain by choosing God!

Say, for instance, that someone shook you when you were little—a mistake some adults made, just trying to quieten a child. They didn't realize this causes damage similar to whiplash. So now when your baby won't stop crying, you might, automatically, start to grab him or her. You might even have your hands poised over the crib or already clutching your child's shoulders. But before anything happens, you suddenly let go. Or, perhaps, a thought rushes into your mind, saying, "This could hurt the baby."

Somehow, God finds a way to speak to you! That's one of His jobs as your Heavenly Father. As His child, your job is to be willing and ready to listen. So, pay attention to this inner voice which quietly speaks to you. Let its power break the chain of events that links one generation's deeds to the next. Let your Redeemer redeem your family and regenerate the generations to come—starting right now with you.

Prayer: Lord, I release to You known and unknown sins I've received from generations past. Let them stop here! Free my ancestors and descendants from any choice, word, or deed that displeases You. I accept Your forgiveness and restoration of my family with thanksgiving and praise of Jesus' name.

Journey with God: If God brings to mind any recollection of abuse, release those situations and persons to Him as you ask for the forgiving, transforming power of Jesus Christ.

_____

_____

_____

_____

_____

_____

_____

Day 67

You give me a better way to live, so I live as you want me to.

Psalm 18:36, NCV

If you didn't like the way a family member reared you, it's not up to you to criticize, blame, or judge! However, it is up to you to decide differently! It's up to you to make a choice to follow God instead of people as you ask His help in bringing up your child.

Before you toss aside everything you've been taught, though, you might question if that's best! Just because an adult family member seemed insensitive to your wants, needs, thoughts, or feelings when you were a child doesn't mean you can't value a single thing that person says. To know what to hold on to—and what to toss aside—you need a reference point to guide you. Since you've chosen God as the center from which all other beliefs radiate or flow, you need to know what you believe about Him!

For example, if you see your Heavenly Father as handling His children harshly, you might be inclined to do the same. If you see Him as creating the whole world then abandoning it, that would also influence your thinking.

Throughout the ages, people have often confined God to their own experiences or the conclusions they reached after hearing about the experiences of other people. To avoid such preconception or misconception, you have to see for

First Days of Parenting

yourself what God's Word says in its entirety and also what it shows you about God, especially through His Son, Jesus Christ. Jesus' life, death, and resurrection reveal full truth about the Heavenly Father: He demonstrates forgiveness and mercy. He gives unending love and power but judges those who will not listen! The fullness of Christ gives a whole and holy view of parenting for you to follow. Through His Spirit, God gives you a better way to live—in *His* best, not yours!

Prayer: Heavenly Father, thank You for showing me the way through Your Son, Jesus. In His holy name and Spirit, help my family to live as You want us to.

Journey with God: List family practices that once bothered you or that you now question. Discuss each with God.

_____

_____

_____

_____

_____

_____

_____

_____

Day 68

And if it seem evil unto you to serve the LORD, choose you this day whom ye will serve; whether the gods which your fathers served that were on the other side of the flood, or the gods of the Amorites, in whose land ye dwell: but as for me and my house, we will serve the LORD.

Joshua 24:15, KJV

"But, that's how we always did things in our family."

"Yeah? Well, I don't like it! It just doesn't seem like a good idea to me."

When two people come together as parents, they bring to their child two sets of values that may not be a matching pair! From their own childhoods, each parent has been given certain training, background, and culture that they either do or don't want to incorporate into parenting. This can make them unsure of themselves and also in conflict with a spouse.

Parenting brings paradox as two very different people try to forge one set of values for their family. Even if they come from the same neighborhood or the same town, had the same friends and basic experiences, or went to the same church and school, they still won't see everything the same way. One set of eyes, ears, lips, or nostrils will not always perceive exactly what another person saw, heard, tasted, or smelled!

As you and your spouse try to adjust your perceptions, priorities, and expectations to each other, you may feel as though you're seeing double! Your values may seem blurred, especially as you first begin to see yourselves as parents. Yet, even if you're bringing up your child alone, you still have the conflict of aligning worldly values in God's sight!

Like prescription lenses, God's Word adjusts a double view of parenting to fit His vision of and for you! The Bible doesn't offer rose-colored glasses but a frame within which to place each perspective. You bring parenting into focus and receive a realistic, single view by choosing one God whom you will serve.

Prayer: Dear God, our standards came from the world and the places in which we grew up and dwelled. That's what we know! That's what we have! But we don't want to serve old habits; we want to serve You. This day, we choose to offer ourselves and our family to You in Jesus' name.

Journey with God: Is anything keeping you and your house from serving the Lord?

_____

_____

_____

_____

_____

_____

_____

Day 69

*I praise the LORD because
he advises me.
Even at night,
I feel his leading.*

Psalm 16:7, NCV

Have you ever noticed how strong leaders in the social, political, or business community often show confidence in themselves and what they're doing? Usually they're not too easily swayed by what others believe or think but seem more inclined to follow their own thoughts, beliefs, or instincts.

In these first days of parenting, you won't always feel particularly confident! If you have inner conflicts about your set of values—or have outer conflicts with a spouse—you'll feel pretty unsure of yourself at times. Although you have decided to follow God, you won't always be 100 percemt sure of what He wants!

As you come up against something in parenting that God's Word doesn't specifically address, take that as His word to listen! Tell Him what's bothering you. Discuss any confusion you feel. Then, wait for Him to speak so you can hear.

In quiet times of waiting to know God's will, praise Him for being with you. Thank Him for His guidance over you and your child. Trust Him to bring to your mind a Bible verse, a memory, or an insight that relates to your present situation.

First Days of Parenting

To answer your questions about parenting, God probably won't give you a set of encyclopedic instructions! He's more apt to bring you an impression or indication of a particular step you're to take. When you've obeyed Him by acting on that information, He'll let you know what's next!

Thank Him for being ever-present. Praise Him for caring about your family. Listen for His loving counsel and advice. In the stillness of a night or the quiet of a waking moment, He'll open your eyes to His personal answer. He'll bring His thoughts and beliefs for you to follow with confidence and strength. He will give you His instinct to love!

Prayer: Heavenly Father, thank You for speaking to me and answering me in accordance with Your will. Help me to grow more confident in my ability to hear You in Jesus' name.

Journey with God: In what ways do you feel led by the Holy Spirit? If you're unsure, focus on times you felt certain of God's will for you. What clues or assurances did you have?

_____

_____

_____

_____

_____

_____

_____

> *I will pay attention to a wise saying;
> I will explain my riddle on the harp.*
>
> Psalm 49:4, NCV

Do you know how to hear God? Just pay attention! Each day He speaks to His children. So, each day His children have to pay attention to be able to hear! In a way, it's like having a twenty-four-hour radio station. You make the decision to turn on the set. You find the right frequency and do what you can to clear the static. But, whether you hear Him very well or not, God continues to speak.

As you begin to recognize His voice more clearly, you'll discover His personal word to you. On rare occasions (usually never!) you might hear Him audibly, but more likely, you'll sense His presence as you become more attuned to Him.

To increase the volume, you can open a Bible translation that's easy for you to "hear" and understand. If you prefer poetic language, you might feel in tune with the *New American Standard* or *King James Version*. If you want a literal translation, try *New Jerusalem* or *New Revised Standard Version*. If you want a conversational time with God, consider *The Amplified Bible, New Century Version,* or *Today's English Version*.

Before opening any Bible, pray for the Holy Spirit to instruct. Then, you may suddenly be drawn to a particular portion of Scripture. Or perhaps, you'll open pages at random and discover the very word you most needed to hear. You might feel urged to investigate a Bible passage that's previously confused you, but this time you'll know just what it means.

God might use also a sermon, hymn, or timely word from a Christian friend to speak to you. He might use a note from nature to remind you that He's there. But, as He speaks, something in you will quieten to listen. You'll feel a sense of peace, a renewed hope, or a clear direction that makes your life sing, harmoniously, with His will.

Prayer: Father, I have so many doubts about myself as a parent. Help me to pay attention to Your Word and what You say to me in Jesus' name.

Journey with God: When you try to hear God, do distractions create static? Could you fine-tune your listening time with frequency or with praise? Ask God what's needed to station you in a position so you can hear better.

_____

_____

_____

_____

_____

_____

Day 71

*Send me your light
and truth to guide me.*

Psalm 43:3, NCV

Most babies don't seem to fear the dark—maybe because they don't catch the evening news or maybe because they don't have to get up and go anywhere! However, you may still need a night-light in your house. Not that you're afraid or anything, but if your baby calls in the middle of a dark and stormy night, you need to see where you're stepping!

As new situations arise in parenting, you might feel as though you're walking around with your lights out! The first time your baby runs a fever, for example, you may have to think through each step slowly to know what to do: (1) Get a rectal thermometer. (2) Coat lightly with white petroleum jelly. (3) Gently insert. (4) Leave in place long enough to get a temperature reading (usually a couple of minutes).

Once you know your baby's temperature, you then consider that information in light of other factors. For instance, you might have noticed a stuffy nose earlier—right after the cat snuck into the nursery. Or maybe you heard that a recent visitor now has a contagious illness, such as the flu.

The facts you gather may seem to bring less illumination than a low-watt night-light! Yet the information may be just enough for the baby's pediatrician to see what's needed. If a similar situation ever arises, you'll then know what to do.

When God calls you to do something, He doesn't expect you to know every step involved; but He will give you enough light to walk in faith and obey. He might bring you a sudden revelation or show a route to take so you can tend your child in a Christlike manner. He might provide assistance through another person who's been lit by His love. However, any light God brings will be reflected in the full truth of His Word.

Prayer: Lord, sometimes I'm afraid of the dark! I'm scared that what I don't know will hurt my baby! Please remove any shadow of fear and give me the light I need in Jesus' name.

Journey with God: What are you afraid of—other people, scary things, yourself? Hold each fear up to Bible truths, relevant to that specific topic.

_____

_____

_____

_____

_____

_____

_____

_____

_____

Day 72

Later, Jesus talked to the people again, saying, "I am the light of the world. The person who follows me will never live in darkness but will have the light that gives life."

John 8:12, NCV

In the streets and alleys of many cities, young people live under boxes or in empty buildings. Some had no choice but to leave behind the darkness of alcoholism, incest, or abuse found at home. Others choose to conceal their fears, hurts, and disappointments by hiding in the drugs and sexual encounters they can easily find on the streets. Yet each "street kid" was once a newborn child.

As a Christian parent, you can't help but wonder how such things came to be. If a sibling or other family member has dropped out of sight or society, you may feel even more concerned about the future of your child. You might ask, "What can I do to keep darkness from prevailing?"

Brevity provides simplistic answers. Yet God's Word clearly addresses the issue. John 1:4–5 says, "In him [Jesus] was life, and the life was the light of all people. The light shines in the darkness, and the darkness did not overcome it" (NRSV). In John 9:5, Jesus says, "As long as I am in the world, I am the light of the world" (NRSV).

You can't predict what your child or others will choose or what they'll do to shut themselves in darkness, but you can accept the light Christ brings to you. Hide nothing from Him! Expose your mistakes and sins. Let Him bring to light anything that's harmful or destructive in your family. Look to Him to show you how to bring up your child in His light.

In Him, you will find light humor and lightened concerns for the present. You'll find lightweightedness about the past and lightheartedness for the future. You will find the Holy Spirit's illumination to guide you as you guide your child.

Prayer: O, God, always bring me Your light in Christ!

Journey with God: Consider your family or Christian community in the light of Christ—and in the light of God's Word.

Day 73

And be not conformed to this world: but be ye transformed by the renewing of your mind, that ye may prove what is that good, and acceptable, and perfect, will of God.

Romans 12:2, KJV

Have you ever had a storm or accident blow a transformer or pull down the electrical lines to your house? When power goes out, so do the lights.

As a Christian, you can expect God's power to come to you through a charism, or gift of the Holy Spirit. Even when churches seem to be poles apart, the transformer—Almighty God—supplies the spiritual connection needed so that no one needs to get hung up on denominational lines!

In the twelfth chapters of Romans and 1 Corinthians, you'll find a list of these gifts, such as a gift of wisdom, mercy, healing, teaching, or cheerfulness. Each gift has one power source: God. Each gift has one purpose: to build up Christ's body, the Church.

While you're in these first days of parenting, you may feel as though you don't have time to be much more than a fingernail in the body of Christ! However, as part of Christ's body, your family can be nurtured and strengthened by the Church. In turn, you can be a stronger fingernail—in the Christian community and in your family too—by receiving the special gift that God brings to you.

Maybe you don't know in what ways you're gifted by the Holy Spirit. Maybe you have more than one gift. But as

God reveals Himself more fully to you, you'll find transforming power at work in you—not to conform you to this world, but to transform your mind through the light of Christ.

Prayer: Heavenly Father, thank You for the empowering gift of Your Holy Spirit given to me through the Lord, Jesus Christ. Help me to see Your light always at work, bringing glory to Your name.

Journey with God: Has a spiritual storm or physical accident jolted you away from God's power? Ask Him how you can get reconnected to Him, His Word, and His Church.

The child grew and became strong, filled with wisdom; and the favor of God was upon him.

Luke 2:40, NRSV

Do you know why Christians need to go to church? To worship God! You can do that somewhat by yourself at home, but most people don't! Some just forget. Some don't know how to worship and praise God by themselves. Some lack routines, commitment, or the sense of discipline that regular churchgoing can bring.

Your church attendance encourages others who come. Your presence blesses them; theirs blesses you. It's hard enough being a Christian parent without trying to do the job alone! It's hard enough just being a Christian! But as you worship within the body of Christ, you have fellowship with others who exhibit belief in God.

To be brought up strong in the Lord, your baby needs embodiment in Christ's body. Right now, it's probably true that only your company really matters, but that means your choices matter most too! So, bring your son or daughter into contact with Christians who love, support, correct, instruct, and bless your child.

By making church attendance an early and ongoing part of your baby's life, you also help to influence future decisions he or she will make. You set an example, demonstrate values, and provide an environment of godly wisdom, truth, and love.

Sometimes, you might think, "My baby is better off at home!" You may feel he or she won't get very much out of going to a church nursery. But surrounded by people who care about God and your child, your son or daughter will learn of trust. Your baby will have every advantage for growing up, spiritually strong, in the Lord.

Prayer: Dear God, thank You for favoring us with Your Son and those who gather in His name to worship You.

Journey with God: Pray for those in your church who work in the nursery or church school department. Ask God what type of involvement you're to have and when.

I sing to the LORD because he has taken care of me.

Psalm 13:6, NCV

The songs your baby hears in the church nursery can set the tempo for music at home. As you sing, "Jesus Loves Me," or other hymns young children like, you make a connection between the places that house your family and your church. Your baby won't think, "Yeah! I've heard that song before!" but he or she can feel the comfort of a familiar tune.

Such ties help to create a loving, supportive bond that strengthens you in bringing up your child in a Christ-like manner. As you go about your day, it's difficult to feel down or be fussy when songs, such as "Amazing Grace" or "Jesus Loves the Little Children," play in the background! Besides mood-setting, appropriate hymns can strike a responsive chord in the youngest heart. Although your child won't yet comprehend the lyrics to a song, he or she can be nurtured by biblical or prayerful words. Just as your baby will eventually recognize certain sounds and voices, so will godly music help to awaken spiritual senses.

You can also show your child—from an early age—how to sing love songs to the Lord! Existing hymns of praise and worship set a beat for you to follow. But, as you read the

Bible, you'll find words that linger and console your spirit or speak with such accord, you just want to harmonize!

So, sing! Don't be concerned about your voice range or musical aptitude! Find the key note and go from there: "I sing to the Lord because He has taken care of me." At any age, that's cause for rejoicing—in worship and in song!

Prayer: Heavenly Father, help me to recall Your love for me and my family through songs of praise in Jesus' name.

Journey with God: Do you feel off-key—as though you're out of tune with God? Has anything stopped the music or kept you from making a joyful noise? Ask God how you can recover your spiritual sense of rhythm, set to His heartbeat.

Day 76

You have taught children and babies to sing praises to you.

Psalm 8:2, NCV

"Coo-che-coo. Ga-ga! Goo."

Do you feel silly using baby talk? Would you feel that way if you knew of scientific studies revealing baby talk as a form of prenatal communication with the mother's body and/or an expression of intimate conversation with God?

Maybe you'll find evidence to that effect. Maybe you won't! However, you will see baby talk discarded as your child develops language skills appropriate to your culture. This comes from hearing words, phrases, and expressions in your native tongue.

Meanwhile, your son or daughter has an ability you may have lost! Your baby can create voice inflections and sounds used by every language on earth! Silent consonants, hissing syllables, and rolling Rs that tripped your tongue when you practiced another language aren't the least bit foreign to your child!

So, here's a thought: Instead of initiating baby talk, let your child teach you some forgotten sounds! Listen then try to repeat. Mimic as well as you can but keep the game playful by smiling and having fun.

When you're the one to start a speaking game, use "real words." Enunciate clearly. Identify any objects to which you refer by pointing to them. Include abstract words too, such as *love, like, happy,* or *sad*—taking care to express the present mood in positive terms and an accepting tone. State simply and often the truths you want to teach your child: "I love you! Jesus loves you!" From the beginning, your words and ways can encourage your baby to sing praise to God.

Prayer: Holy Father, thank You for the language of Your love, given to my family in Christ's name.

Journey with God: Have you gotten in the habit of speaking in a manner that's foreign to God? Ask Him how your choice of words can edify others and bring praise to Him.

_____

_____

_____

_____

_____

_____

_____

_____

_____

_____

And how from infancy you have known the holy Scriptures, which are able to make you wise for salvation through faith in Christ Jesus.

2 Timothy 3:15, NIV

"But I've always known _____."

From the moment of birth, a child begins to learn. Some suspect that learning begins even earlier, and, occasionally, that's shown to be true. For example, an unwanted baby might be born "just knowing" there's no welcome. When a parent prays for a child in the womb, the infant might enter the world with a highly developed interest in knowing God.

Most babies and children learn quickly. However, few can be easily un-taught! Information can later be corrected and thoughts or actions redirected; but, frankly, what's there is there! This can cause a child to feel confused, resentful, or discouraged from wanting to learn anything more!

What you tell your child now is what he or she will know to be true. For example, if you refer to your spouse as "Mom" or "Dad," that's the word choice your baby will eventually follow. If you later discover that *Mama, Mother, Ma, Daddy, Pa, Pappy,* or *Papa* is preferred, you could be in trouble! Or your baby may wonder, "Who *is* this person anyway?"

Your word choices and tone will also affect your child's thoughts and beliefs about God. What you say might not have much impact at the moment, but your expressions and attitudes will foster interest. Soon, your baby will begin to notice how you sound when you mention Jesus' name or how you hold the Bible when you read. From early infancy, your daughter or son can know there's something special about the Scriptures—and the blessed name of God.

Prayer: Dear Father, thank You for drawing me and my family to Your Word in Jesus' name.

Journey with God: Is your understanding of the Bible the same as it was in childhood? Ask God to bring to your attention Scriptures that will help your faith mature in Him.

All scripture is inspired by God and is useful for teaching, for reproof, for correction, and for training in righteousness, so that everyone who belongs to God may be proficient, equipped for every good work.

2 Timothy 3:16–17, NRSV

Do you feel equipped to be a parent? As you continue your time of devotional reading, journaling, and praying, you'll become more and more proficient in this job! You'll realize that—because you belong to God—His Word, His Son, and His Holy Spirit belong to you! So how could you possibly go wrong? How could you ever be inept?

Actually, committed Christians can become inadequate as parents! How? They can lose their "equipment" by losing their commitment to a Christ-centered family. Usually, that doesn't happen overnight but over time as people overextend themselves. Or, perhaps, a crisis becomes a focal point for a family's life. However, as you continue to spend time with the Lord each day, you needn't worry about forgetting Him!

Parental inadequacies can also arise from simple misunderstanding about the meaning of God's Word or content of a personal message. For example, people might insist, "I *know* what God said to me!" No doubt, they do. Yet this does not mean there's nothing more to learn! God's Word is living! It doesn't die on the spot of someone's understanding! It continues to reveal and unfold itself, more and more fully, throughout your life—and throughout your child's life too.

Right now, your baby can't pick up a Bible, much less read what it says. But, even young infants can hold onto the lightweight, vinyl-coated or cloth books that bring Scripture to them. Colorful pictures illustrate Bible thoughts or texts of a verse or two. So, increase proficiency in your family! Equip yourselves by holding onto God and His Word.

Prayer: Heavenly Father, sometimes I feel like an infant, trying to comprehend Your Word! In Jesus' name, I ask You to breathe Your Holy Spirit into each page as I read.

Journey with God: Has something in the Bible put you off by its reproof or correction? Don't let this put off your best equipment for parenting! Tell God how you feel. Let Him train your thoughts toward His good work in you!

_____

_____

_____

_____

_____

_____

_____

God, we have heard about you. Our ancestors told us what you did in their days, in days long ago.

Psalm 44:1, NCV

Aren't holidays great? Remember how much you enjoyed Christmas, Easter, and birthdays when you were little? Now you'll regain that delight as you spend your first holidays with your child!

The customs you begin start a pageantry of special occasions. So, think about the traditions handed down to you and your spouse. Prayerfully consider what you believe you're to include in your family's celebrations and what you feel you're to omit.

The pages of the Bible are rich with customs, traditions, and instructions concerning various occasions. Maybe you've heard about these most of your life, but why not find out for yourself? Before your family's first holidays begin, why not read Bible accounts of how these holy-days got started? Then be alert to any impressions you receive about a custom you're to add or drop. Talk with your spouse about this. Find out what means the most or has been particularly important to him or her. If your favorite moments or experiences coincide, you might want to incorporate these into your present celebration. But don't assume it's okay! Ask God!

Talk with the Lord about customs that may or may not be pleasing to Him. Pray about each one, asking Him to help you to agree. If you're celebrating alone with your child, ask God to urge you in the holiday direction you're to go. Let Him guide you in a holy, joyous, Christ-centered celebration!

Prayer: Dear God, just because our families observed holidays a certain way as we were growing up doesn't mean that pleases You. Help us to know how and when You want us to proclaim Your gifts and announce a celebration in Christ's name.

Journey with God: Ask God what would make each special occasion in your family truly special to Him.

> *His anger lasts only a moment, but his kindness lasts for a lifetime. Crying may last for a night, but joy comes in the morning.*
>
> Psalm 30:5, NCV

Have you had the joy of sleeping through the night? As your household begins to settle into uninterrupted sleep, you may think, "Ah! Peace at last!" But, don't count on it!

Placing expectations on your baby can be a source of frustration or annoyance. However, it helps to know what to expect in general. For instance, as your baby nears four to six months of age, you can look for signs of teething. Gums may seem red or swollen. Frequent drooling may begin. And those sleepless nights may reappear!

Some babies teethe with hardly any discomfort. But, the strongest, toughest teeth can have difficulty cutting through the strongest, toughest gums! What seems to be the cutting edge of a problem might actually be a blessing!

Books and articles on child development can let you know about teething and other general stages to expect, but they can't tell you exactly *when* each will occur. Guidelines keep you informed and better prepared to handle situations that arise, but don't expect your baby's growth to go by any book!

Your child is unique—an individual like every other baby, yet like none! Therefore, you can expect a unique set of circumstances to surround each "normal" pattern of growth. For example, your baby might suddenly fuss or cry until dawn, then seem just fine! Call the doctor if you like; but, unless other symptoms develop, the pediatrician may not be able to diagnose anything, except perhaps to say, "Your baby had an off-day." That's to be expected occasionally, but who can guess when off-days will occur? You can, however, know this: God's favor rests upon you and your baby. Day by day, night by night, His kindness lasts a lifetime—and beyond!

Prayer: Dear Father, help me not to take You or my family for granted. Please remove any false expectations from us, and give us joyful growth in You in Jesus' name.

Journey with God: Think about what you expect from yourself, your baby, and your family. What do you expect from God?

Day 81

*"Be still, and know that I am God;
I will be exalted among the nations,
I will be exalted in the earth."*

Psalm 46:10, NIV

Are you starting to see your baby as a little night owl or an early bird? Most likely, your son or daughter has begun to establish a sleeping pattern that could last a lifetime! From infancy, people usually show a strong preference, either for staying up late and sleeping late or going to bed early and arising at the first blink of dawn. As long as your baby settles into a routine that coincides with yours, no problem! However, your child may prefer the opposite, so one of you winds up being chronically tired.

Changing an overall sleep-pattern—yours or your baby's—can be difficult. Neither of you wants to be uncooperative, but each family member feels more alert at some hours of the day or evening than others—which may not be too negotiable!

To work out a routine that adjusts to everyone in the house, consider energy cycles of each person throughout the day or night. For example, when you first awaken, do you feel groggy or clear-headed? After lunch, do you have pep or need a nap? Do you slump before or after dinner? Do you burst with energy at bedtime or fall asleep on the sofa?

As you ask similar questions of each family member, you will find solutions! If a long afternoon nap keeps your baby awake when you really really want to go to bed, you'll know to decrease the length of nap times—or take an afternoon nap yourself! As you evaluate each option in the light of each individual's needs, you'll find a workable but unique schedule for your whole family.

So, don't get ruffled about sleep patterns! Be still! Remember, you can enjoy the quiet company of God any time— night or day. Shhh. . . . Listen, and you will hear.

Prayer: Lord, I didn't expect it to be such a big deal to coordinate schedules to include simple necessities—like sleep! Help me to know my family's needs and find solutions. Please quieten me to hear You well in Jesus' name.

Journey with God: Do you feel like exalting God in the middle of the night or first thing in the morning? Talk with Him about your personal needs. Listen to what He personally wants from you!

_____

_____

_____

_____

_____

_____

Day 82

Even children make themselves known by their acts, by whether what they do is pure and right.

Proverbs 20:11, NRSV

Healthy babies can usually make themselves heard! A whimper, yell, squeal, or wail will get an adult's attention! But, soon, the gloriously sweet sound of laughter will make your baby's delight known too.

Some babies don't ever seem to smile. They look grumpy, even when they're not! Some seem impish. Others perpetually jut a lower lip while still others always grin. Some babies look as though everything holds their interest. Others seem to say, "Yeah, I see what's going on, but don't expect me to let anyone know."

Occasionally, parents feel disappointed. They think their baby is "wrong" to be a certain way, so they try to force changes to fit their expectations. They don't realize that the only changes an infant needs is a change of diapers, a change of diet, or a change of sleeping positions!

As children begin to understand right from wrong, they might choose to rebel or misbehave. Then, loving parents will need to correct and change—not the child's individuality, but any poor choices or behavior the individual makes.

Your baby's personality presents your family with a wondrous gift—a priceless gift that's never meant to be exchanged! This mental, physical, and emotional disposition provides a unique and very personal identity that's like other people, yet like no one else. So, enjoy it! Accept it! And you will accept your child.

Prayer: Heavenly Father, thank You for the lovely makeup you gave my child. Help me to accept the gift of this wondrous personality in Jesus' name.

Journey with God: Do you wish your baby seemed happier, quieter, more alert, or _____? (Fill in the blank.) Discuss any disappointments with God, asking Him to help you change your expectations.

_____

_____

_____

_____

_____

_____

_____

_____

_____

_____

Day 83

Fathers, do not exasperate your children; instead, bring them up in the training and instruction of the Lord.

Ephesians 6:4, NIV

In a traditional Judeo-Christian family, comprised of father, mother, and child, the man holds the place as "head of the house." No one knows *exactly* what God had in mind! However, it's usually true that when you put a bunch of people together in one house, somebody needs to be in charge.

Male or female, if you're the head of your household, there's a price on your head! God knows you have a heady position! He knows how easily you can impose your thoughts, will, and expectations your family. So, He makes a point of saying something to this effect: *Don't train your child to fit yourself but to BE fit in the Lord.*

To do that without having fits, you need to know what God wants. You can't possibly train your child in His ways without knowing what those ways are. You can't instruct anyone in the Lord without first learning what He's teaching you. So, instead of being a source of pride, your position as head of your household can be humbling! Instead of holding authority over everyone in your family, you've found yourself under the direct headship and authority of God.

As the person who's most responsible for your family, you'll be blessed as you train yourself to respond to God. Read His Word. Look to Him to guide you. Let Him speak to you through the words, thoughts, and feelings of each person in your house. As you—the head of your household—seek the Lord, your body of family members will eventually follow you as they seek Him too!

Prayer: Dear God, sometimes I'd just like for everyone in my family to do what I want when I want it! But that's often heady or heavy. I don't want to be in charge! I want You to be our one authority with Jesus Christ as the Head. Help us to go by His family name.

Journey with God: Who has the power in your family? Talk with God about the power of His Holy Spirit, given to you through Christ.

_____

_____

_____

_____

_____

_____

_____

_____

Day 84

> But if we have food and clothing,
> we will be content with that.
>
> 1 Timothy 6:8, NIV

A contented baby.... That's what loving parents want! That's usually what they get, too, as their infant matures enough to rest well, outgrow colic, and digest solid foods. Your baby may have already reached this stage or soon will. So, as you add solid foods to the daily menu, introduce them one at a time with a few days between each new entree. If you suspect your child will be inclined to have any food allergies, just wait a little longer—perhaps a week to ten days—before adding the next food.

For starters, most doctors recommend cooked cereal grain mixed thin with formula. Oats, barley, and rice usually incur fewer allergic reactions than wheat. However, you'll probably find that each parent's likes and dislikes give you some clue about foods your baby will be able to accept.

When your baby is ready for fruits and vegetables, you might not like seeing unknown ingredients listed on baby food labels! You might have noted that preservatives don't set well with other members of your family, or maybe you just want your baby to have foods closer to their natural state.

As you check into the options, consider a reasonably inexpensive, preservative-free alternative that takes little preparation time—assuming that you eat nutritiously! As you boil or microwave your own dinner, add enough for your baby. Omit any oil and seasonings until you've removed a baby-sized, cooked portion. Then put that in a food blender, or mash well and strain.

As your baby first tastes something new, food may fly across the room! If this happens each time you try a certain food, take that as a definite, "Yuck! Let's find something else!" But God is so good! He created such a variety of food, tastes, and textures, you'll surely find ones your baby likes!

Prayer: Heavenly Father, thanks for the colorful assortments You bring to us! Thanks for considering individual tastes!

Journey with God: Are you content with what God has provided you? Do you want more than you have? Talk with God about your partiality for certain food, clothes, or material goods.

Day 85

This is what I want: Let me live in the LORD's house all my life.

Psalm 27:4, NCV

Assuming there's a roof over your head, are you thinking about one that covers more square footage? Most people want additional space as their families expand. But, before you make a decision, prayerfully consider each alternative.

Ask yourself, for example, where, when, and how much extra space you need. Would an older home be a better buy or more affordable than a brand new house? Could you make the needed repairs or improvements yourself? Would enclosing a porch or adding onto your present dwelling provide you with a workable solution?

Prayerfully consider present priorities and future possibilities too. For instance, if cramped living quarters have been a source of annoyance or inconvenience, a primary consideration now will be space. However, if you also have concerns about your school district, your location will be a higher priority as your child nears kindergarten age.

As you consider what's important to you and your family, be specific and realistic. For example, if you know you would like to live in a nicer neighborhood, ask yourself, "How will our budget be affected, not just in terms of money, but also time?" If you decide to stay put and add onto your home, ask, "Which tasks can we do ourselves, and which will require a contractor?" Again, think about how many hours and dollars you will need to commit to the work.

Whether you decide to move up, across town, or nowhere new, make the Lord's house—your church—your top housing priority! Visit it often. Pray for the place and the people. Let your church become your family's real home.

Prayer: Heavenly Father, thank You for giving us a dwelling place with You, no matter where we are. Thank You for Your Church. Help us always to be at home there in Jesus' name.

Journey with God: Pray for your church, pastor, and people who gather in Christ's name. Ask God to help you know His housing priorities for your family.

_____

_____

_____

_____

_____

_____

_____

_____

Day 86

In the Lord's name, I tell you this. Do not continue living like those who do not believe. Their thoughts are worth nothing. They do not understand, and they know nothing, because they refuse to listen. So they cannot have the life that God gives.

Ephesians 4:17–18, NCV

Okay, be honest. Do you want a nicer, bigger, better house in a nicer, bigger, better neighborhood because that would be nice and better for your family as it gets bigger? Or, do you want to keep up with the proverbial Joneses? Do you want to impress people—your boss, parents, or friends? As young adults begin to build their family, reputation, and careers, they often want to show others, "Hey! Look at me! I can do this adult stuff pretty well!" That's to be expected as they also try to build confidence in themselves and their ability to handle adult responsibilities.

Danger comes, however, in trying to live up to standards set by someone else. Trying hard to compete, prove yourself, or live up to expectations placed on you by family, work, or friends can trap you in a life of resentment, disappointment, and, ultimately, failure. Yet, throughout the country, that's what many people do.

As you bring up your family, constantly seek a better way—the life that God gives. At times, it won't seem nicer or more desirable, yet you will succeed in having your needs met. You'll know who you are and where you're going, and you won't have to prove that to anyone!

By putting God first, you don't have to be concerned about pleasing people but pleasing Him. The life He brings your family will be more than pleasing to you!

Prayer: Heavenly Father, help me to put You first—not just in daily thoughts and decisions but in a lifetime goal of seeking You. Please remind me when I forget, and give me the discernment I need to recognize choices that I didn't even know I had! Help me to choose Your life for me and my family in Jesus' holy name.

Journey with God: It's so much easier to follow what everyone else is doing than to find out what God wants. But don't let that stop you now! Ask Him about the individual and family life He's planned for you.

_____

_____

_____

_____

_____

_____

_____

_____

_____

Day 87

*Except the LORD build the house,
they labour in vain that build it:
except the LORD keep the city,
the watchman waketh but in vain.*

Psalm 127:1, KJV

Naturally, you want a safe neighborhood for your family! Every loving parent does! But, to provide that, have you been thinking about taking an extra job—one that would keep you too busy to see your baby? Or, have you considered just going ahead and moving into a place you can't afford? That's tempting, especially if you feel your family's safety is at stake. But is it?

Whether you're in a fancy neighborhood or an inner-city area that's seen better days, God is able to protect your home from intruders. He's your watchman and your guard! You can rely on His ability to sound an alarm so you can hear—assuming, of course, that you've chosen to listen!

As God provides your family protection, He may urge you to move. Or, maybe He'll encourage you to stay where you are and get an alarm system or a dog. He might even help you to appreciate the neighborhood you're in but warn you about the dangers inside your own house!

For instance, He may help you to notice frayed cords, tipsy lamps, unprotected outlets, or faulty wiring. He might remind you to get a smoke detector or a fire extinguisher. Or, maybe He'll give you an impression of some actions

First Days of Parenting

you can take to "baby proof" your home before your child crawls or becomes more mobile.

So, don't keep watch in vain! Watch for the Lord! He knows your needs. He cares about your safety. He alone can build your home into a secure place where He can dwell!

Prayer: Lord, all the worrying I do about my family is a vain effort, isn't it? Help me to trust You to protect and build us together in a manner worthy of Christ's name.

Journey with God: Do you get the impression that God is trying to warn you or tell you something important? Listen. Note what comes to mind.

___

___

___

___

___

___

___

___

___

___

___

Day 88

It is no use for you to get up early and stay up late, working for a living. The LORD gives sleep to those he loves. Children are a gift from the LORD; babies are a reward.

Psalm 127:2–3, NCV

Does someone in your house work for a living? If so, great! God's Word encourages honest, honorable work, showing it to be a blessing. However, the Bible discourages workers from wearing themselves out. It's no use to get up earlier and earlier or go to bed later and later to finish what needs doing! It accomplishes nothing except, perhaps, to show that something's wrong!

God can help you see any flaws in your values. He can reveal your motives and the truth. He can help you set godly priorities that put Him first, then your family, then your work. Since work includes time, energy, and attention on the job, around the house, in your church, in the local community, or throughout the whole world, you need to be sure what your job is. Otherwise, you may be doing someone else's!

To find out, you might consider if you're losing sleep over anything. Or, ask yourself if you're letting some task or personal pleasure get in the way of your relationship with God, your family, or your church. If so, you'll need His help in untangling your involvements and getting your priorities aligned with His.

First Days of Parenting

God doesn't want you to lose sleep, trying to guess what He wants from you! He wouldn't be a very kind parent if He played those kinds of games. He'll let you know what you're to do by giving you a sense of peace about it—a peace that lets you rest in Him. After all, He is your Heavenly Father. So, as His child, your life is a gift to Him.

Prayer: Thank You, Father, for accepting me into the precious gift of Your family in Jesus' name.

Journey with God: Is something wearing you out? Discuss the details of your situation with God. Listen to the impressions He gives you about any changes you're to make.

> *Lo, children are an heritage of the LORD: and the fruit of the womb is his reward. As arrows are in the hand of a mighty man; so are the children of the youth. Happy is the man that hath his quiver full of them:*
>
> Psalm 127:2–4, KJV

Oh, my, how you've grown these last few weeks! Your baby is delightful too!

Have you captured lots of pictures at each new stage of growth? Have you dated the backs of photographs to remind you how cute your child is at every age and stage? Have you thought about putting another baby in the family picture?

Only you, your spouse, and God can decide when it's time to expand your family. However, His choice may have little to do with a biological time clock! According to the Bible, God's timing for the Jewish nation began many years after Abraham and Sarah supposedly could have children! Then, the birth of Christianity came as Christ was born to a virgin—a bit earlier than people usually expect!

For reasons known to yourself and the Lord, it may be that no more children will be in your family album. However, that doesn't mean no more children in the picture! You may be in a classroom, filled with fresh hopes and children's faces. You may be called to baby-sit a neighbor's child or to provide a home for a niece or nephew.

As your baby grows up, you might find yourself called "Mom" or "Dad" by friends brought home to meet you. You might decide to adopt a child or give birth to another baby. But, as you keep company with young people, you will be truly blessed. The seriousness, laughter, and unique perspectives of children bring such wondrous rewards, you'll probably stay younger longer, just being with them!

Prayer: Dear God, please help me not to become set in my ways but in Yours in Jesus' name.

Journey with God: Ask God to give you His view of your family and the young people He pictures you as loving.

_____

_____

_____

_____

_____

_____

_____

_____

_____

_____

_____

Day 90

*Glorify the LORD with me,
and let us praise his name together.*

Psalm 34:3, NCV

If you have the blessed company of a Christian spouse or friend with whom you pray, glorify the Lord together! Praise Him for the family to whom you've committed your love in the family name of Christ.

As your baby grows, you'll continue to have new concerns to face and new decisions to make. Because you love your child, you'll always want what's best, and that's what you'll find as you seek God and pray.

If you have a regular prayer partner, you'll encourage each other's faith in God and commitment to Him. But, even if you think you're alone, you're not! You'll see God's wisdom and love come to you, again and again, as things you wouldn't have thought of by yourself suddenly spring to mind!

God is with you in word and truth and prayer. His Holy Spirit will prevail as you ask His help in bringing up your child. So, seek Him always in the power and prayer of Jesus, who teaches you to love and pray.

Prayer: Our Father, who from heaven looks out for my family, let Your name become most holy in our lives. Let Your kingdom come into my home, church, and community. Let Your will be done and carried on in my family, just as it always is in heaven. Give us this day everything we need to work, play, rest, and worship You. Forgive me for letting expectations get in the way of what You want and for trespassing against the rights or feelings of others. Help me to forgive, even if my family expects too much or too little of me, and lead me not into the temptation of following what other people say or do. Deliver me from the evil of thinking I'm the best parent or the worst! Give me the peace and joy that comes from being in the ever-present company of Your kingdom. Let my love for You, my family, and Your Church grow in Your power and for Your glory, forever, in Christ's name.

Journey with God: Ask God to help you personalize the Lord's Prayer for your family. Seek Him in journaling and journeying with God in the wondrous days of parenting yet to come!

_____

_____

_____

_____

_____

_____

_____

First Days of Parenting

First Days of Parenting

First Days of Parenting

First Days of Parenting

First Days of Parenting

First Days of Parenting

First Days of Parenting

First Days of Parenting

First Days of Parenting

First Days of Parenting

First Days of Parenting

First Days of Parenting

First Days of Parenting

First Days of Parenting

First Days of Parenting

First Days of Parenting

First Days of Parenting

First Days of Parenting

First Days of Parenting